BOOK REVIEWS AND
"HOW AMERICA W ...ULD"

1. THE SCRANTON TRIBUNE, THURSDAY OCTOBER 5ᵀᴴ, 2000.

TRUCKSVILLE MAN WRITES REGIONS FINANCIAL HISTO-RY BOOK. IN THE BOOK, HE TRACES THE HISTORY OF THE ANTHRACITE INDUSTRY FROM THE EARLY 1800'S, BUT HE ALSO EXPLAINS THE WORK IS MORE THAN JUST A RECOUNTING OF HISTORICAL FACTS. "IT'S REALLY A NOVEL THAT EXPLAINS WHAT HAPPENED TO THE PEO-PLE OF NORTHEASTERN PENNSYLVANIA DUE TO THE BUSINESS DEALINGS OF THE COAL BARONS AND INDUS-TRIALIST J. P. MORGAN. THE BOOKS MAJOR PREMISE CENTERS ON HOW MORGAN FINANCED MANY OF HIS HIGH STAKES BUSINESS DEALS BY ACCESSING NORTHEASTERN PENNSYLVANIA COAL MONEY.

2. TUDOR BOOK STORE, KINGSTON, PENNSYLVANIA.

THE AUTHOR HAS CREATED AN INTERPRETIVE DOCU-MENT DETAILING THE CONTRIBUTIONS OF NORTHEAST PENNSYLVANIA TO THE GREATNESS OF THE UNITED STATES OF AMERICA RESULTING IN AN ECONOMIC, FINANCIAL, AND POLITICAL REVITALIZATION OF THE UNITED STATES OF AMERICA.

3. THE DALLAS POST, DALLAS, PA JANUARY 10, 2001.

THE BIRTHPLACE OF THE AMERICAN INDUSTRIAL REVOLUTION WAS THE WYOMING VALLEY AND NORTHEASTERN PENNSYLVANIA, ACCORDING TO A NEWLY PUBLISHED BOOK WRITTEN BY A LOCAL RESIDENT. THE BOOK CONTAINS FACTS ABOUT

J. P. MORGAN'S POWER IN THE COAL MINING INDUSTRY
FROM THE LATE 1800'S UNTIL HIS DEATH IN 1913. THE
BOOK EXPLORES HOW MORGAN WAS THE CONTROL-
LING PERSON BEHIND OVER 112 MAJOR CORPORATIONS
THROUGH HIS USE OF PROFITS FROM THE ANTHRACITE
COAL INDUSTRY.

4. THE SCRANTON TIMES, OCTOBER 5TH, 2000.

NORTHEASTERN PENNSYLVANIA MAY HAVE PLAYED A
GREATER ROLE IN THE NATION'S ECONOMIC HISTORY
THAN MOST PEOPLE REALIZE. IN THE BOOK THE
AUTHOR TRACES THE HISTORY OF THE ANTHRACITE
INDUSTRY FROM THE EARLY 1800'S AND THE CIVIL WAR
THROUGH THE TURN OF THE CENTURY AND INTO
WORLD WAR I AND II. MR. DOMBROSKI SAYS HE WROTE
THE BOOK NOT ONLY AS A HISTORICAL REFERENCE BUT
ALSO AS A SOCIAL COMMENTARY. "WE HAVE BEEN IN A
SITUATION FOR MORE THAN 150 YEARS WHERE THE
ECONOMICS HAVE BEEN CONTROLLED BY A SMALL
GROUP OF INDIVIDUALS WHO HAD THEIR OWN SELF
INTEREST AT HEART AND SO NOW WE HAVE TO FORGET
THAT AND REMEMBER WHILE THAT WAS AN IMPEDI-
MENT IT SHOULD NOT BE AN IMPEDIMENT TO THE
FUTURE," HE WRITES.

5. SCRANTON SUNDAY TIMES, NOVEMBER 12, 2000

"SCRANTON AREA BANKS AND WILKES BARRE AREA
BANKS WERE ACTUALLY STARTED BY COAL MINING
INTERESTS TO SERVE THE NEEDS OF THE COAL COL-
LIERIES BEING BUILT," SAYS MR. DOMBROSKI. BECAUSE
MANY OF THE BANKS FORMED IN THE 1800'S WERE
CLOSELY AFFILIATED WITH THE MINING COMPANIES,
THEY ALSO SERVED IN SOME WAYS TO CONTROL AND

OFTEN LIMIT MUCH OF THE AREA'S ECONOMIC GROWTH MR. DOMBROSKI CONTENDS." THE BANKS WERE NEVER RECEPTIVE TO LENDING MONEY TO BUSINESSES, WHICH MIGHT THREATEN THE OPERATION OF THE COAL MINES BY TAKING WORKERS FROM THEM," HE SAID.

HOW AMERICA WAS FINANCED

THIS BOOK REVEALS THE FOLLOWING INFORMATION:

LEARN WHO THE LEAD CONSPIRATOR WAS IN KEEPING MAJOR INDUSTRY OUT OF NORTHEASTERN PENNSYLVANIA DURING AND AFTER THE INDUSTRIAL REVOLUTION.

DISCOVER WHO ELECTED THE SEVEN PRESIDENTS FROM OHIO

FIND OUT WHERE J. P. MORGAN GOT HIS EQUITY AND DEBT CAPITAL.

1. WHY DID TEDDY ROOSEVELT TRY TO SETTLE THE COAL MINE STRIKE IN 1902?
2. WHERE J. P. MORGAN'S MONEY TRUST EXISTED.
3. WHY JOSEPH PULITZER WAS NEVER SUED BY TEDDY ROOSEVELT?
4. WHO PROVIDED TEDDY ROOSEVELT WITH THE SAFARI TO AFRICA?
5. WHO REALLY BUILT THE TRANS CONTINENTAL RAILROAD.
6. WHY BETHLEHEM STEEL WAS NOT INCLUDED IN THE UNITED STATES STEEL CORPORATION?
7. FIND OUT WHERE THE GOLD PROFITS FROM THE WESTERN STRIKE WENT.
8. WHERE THE MONEY CAME FROM TO BUILD THE TRANSCONTINENTAL RAILROAD?
9. WHAT COMMODITY CREATED THE LARGEST MONEY VALUE IN THE UNITED STATES DURING THE LATE 1800'S?
10. WHAT CAUSED THE DEPRESSION IN 1929?
11. WHO FINANCED THOMAS EDISON?
12. WHO FINANCED JOHN D. ROCKEFELLER?

How America Was Financed

How America Was Financed

The True Story of Northeastern Pennsylvania's
Contribution to the Financial and Economic
Greatness of the United States of America

Thomas W. Dombroski

Writers Club Press
San Jose New York Lincoln Shanghai

How America Was Financed

iUniverse books may be ordered through booksellers or by contacting:

iUniverse
1663 Liberty Drive
Bloomington, IN 47403
www.iuniverse.com
1-800-Authors (1-800-288-4677)

ISBN: 978-1-4620-1800-0 (sc)
ISBN: 978-1-4620-1802-4 (e)

Printed in the United States of America

Dedication

*TO MY WIFE NANCY AND MY CHILDREN THOMAS JR.,
SUSAN, JOYCE, AND IN PARTICULAR RONALD WHO
ASSISTED ME IN THE RESEARCH AND PROVIDED ME
WITH CERTAIN DIRECTION TO GET THE FULL STORY
TOGETHER IN A LOGICAL MANNER.*

Contents

List of Illustrations

INDEX TO THE FIGURES AND ILLUSTRATIONS

Foreword

This is not a historical novel yet it is in a sense historical and contained within this book is a true story of how America was financed. While some historical facts weave the story, the players are not necessarily well defined since nearly all business deals, particularly financing situations, are confidential and private.

In order to understand what happened in North East Pennsylvania over the last two hundred years it is necessary to meld history, fact, and speculation. While the names of the movers are correct to the best extent possible, it can not be proven or disputed as to the morality of the actions taken, but the results are there as historical fact for philosophers and historians to judge.

Even the parents and grand parents of the land and coal inheritors could not have known or proven all that took place. In addition, those people who were affected by the actions of the land and coal owners in the North East Pennsylvania did not know what was happening to them and their children and their grandchildren. These people who live today in North East Pennsylvania do not know what the people had to go through to live under the conditions that were present when anthracite coal mining was prominent. Mining coal was the only way for the people to make a living, for the majority of the people, with in the area of North East Pennsylvania and it was arranged that way by those who brought the people to the area for this purpose, to work in the coal mines.

This book is written with the hope that people who now live here in North Eastern Pennsylvania and people in other areas of the United States of America can understand how our area, the coal resources and people contributed to the financial greatness of the United States. Moral judgments as to what happened here and the result is left for other historians to judge.

Preface

The author has created an interpretive document detailing the contributions of North East Pennsylvania to the greatness of the United States of America resulting in an economic, financial, and political revitalization of the United States of America.

The book details the accidental and the deliberate things that were done during the 130 years of the first use of anthracite coal to further the prosperity of few and the enslavement of many.

No other economic factor in the United States. ever resulted in such great prosperity and economic progress as the discovery and usage of anthracite coal. Without the ingenuity of the Connecticut people and the shrewdness in business of J. P. Morgan, the United States would not be the great nation it is today. It is unusual that those who contributed and sacrificed to make this happen benefited the least even to today in northeast Pennsylvania.

Acknowledgements

Thomas Dombroski the author is the youngest (of 9) the son of John and Josephine Dombroski who were immigrants from Poland prior to World War I. His father and mother immigrated in the late 1880s and his father became a coal miner in Northeastern PA until the early 1930s. Nancy Mills Dombroski wife of Thomas is the daughter of Horace and Edna Mills who immigrated from Wales at the turn of the century. Thomas and Nancy have four children Joyce Gebhardt, Susan Irvin, Thomas Jr., and Ronald.

Ronald was instrumental in assisting with the research for this book and providing information that assisted the author in developing the book.

Congressman Kanjorski's staff who provided valuable information from the Library of Congress concerning the 1912 investigation of J. P. Morgan to determine if Morgan had a money trust.

Senator Lemmond for providing information on the creation of the Bureau of Mines and the enactment of coal mine safety laws

The Osterhout library for providing valuable references for further reading and their assistance in providing library of congress information

The Scranton public library for providing information on the library of congress

List of Contributors

Ronald Dombroski assisted in the research and commentary to enable the author to provide to the readers a clear and comprehensive picture of the methods used by few to bring about "through questionable means" the industrial revolution. This resulted in the United States becoming a world economic power through the Connecticut peoples' control of J. P. Morgan and utilizing his financial genius.

Introduction

In 1912 after one year of investigation and countless witnesses and their testimony encompassing 2,226 pages, the Pujo Committee in U.S. Congress could not determine whether J. P. Morgan had a money trust. Nor could they determine how the money trust controlled the 112 plus corporations through J.P. Morgan.

While Morgan was de facto the controlling person behind 112 plus major corporations in the U.S., no one on the committee could pinpoint his source of risk money (capital) or his actual ability and power to control all of these major U.S. corporations. Examples of how J. P. Morgan took control of the various corporations show that Morgan had a strangle hold financially on all of the corporations through the interlocking directorates, control of voting stock through trusts, and the fact that Morgan's banks and investment houses that he controlled had the ability to strangle a corporation financially if the corporate heads did not do his bidding.

Admitting this fact to a congressional committee would be tantamount to committing corporate suicide. Therefore, while the Pujo Committee caused great consternation to Morgan resulting in his death in 1913, they could not pinpoint the source of his financial power as he countered and sidestepped their questions.

His estate when settled in 1916 amounted to less than 100 million while Rockefeller at that time was reported to be worth a billion. Rockefeller made the comment at the funeral of Morgan (and I thought he was a wealthy man) Rockefeller had been financed even to 1916 by the Morgan interests (coal money) and when Rockefeller died his final estate was set at 25 million.

Edison, Carnegie, Dupont, Western Electric, Ford, Westinghouse, the railroads including New York Central and the Transcontinental Union Pacific and others reviewed in this book were financed by Morgan in his financial career. Where could Morgan have obtained the necessary risk equity and capital to finance the start up of all these operations? This is the subject of this book.

It will be shown that Morgan financed all the ventures using the North East Pennsylvania coal trust money that was sent to England and came back through his father Junius until 1890. Each business deal needed Junius' blessing until he died in 1890. From 1890 on J. P. Morgan no longer needed his father's blessing on each venture and the greatest expansion of Industry took place from 1890 through 1913 and J. P. Morgan's demise.

No one (including J. P. Morgan's son) could replace his mastery of finance and control., and his ingenuity in playing one competitor against the other and financing the winner.

Further in 1913, the Federal Reserve came into being and this removed the need for a Morgan because the Federal Reserve now became the central bank of the U.S. To make matters worse the Clayton Antitrust Act came into being looking into all kinds of interlocking trusts. The end result of Morgan's death was a financial shambles of which his son had no concept as to how he could control the corporations as his father had done.

Further, now that J. P. was dead his control over the Dow and his manipulations of stock prices to keep the price of his stocks stable was now gone. This resulted in what was known as the 1929 stock market crash and the resulting depression. In 1929 through 1933 while the country was in financial peril, no apples were sold on the street corners of North Eastern Pennsylvania.

This is the true story of North Eastern Pennsylvania's financial contribution to the financial and economic development of the United States of America.

This is a story of Wyoming Valley and North Eastern Pennsylvania the birth place of the Industrial Revolution.

The Financing of The United States of America

*THE REAL STORY OF ANTHRACITE COALS
PART IN BRINGING ABOUT THE INDUSTRIAL
REVOLUTION IN THE UNITED STATES*

CHAPTER 1

Coal is Discovered and the Die is Cast

Coal is Discovered and the Die is Cast

In order to properly relate to the beginning of the Industrial Revolution and the financing of America, we would have to go back to the discovery of anthracite or hard coal in North Eastern Pennsylvania. It is a historical fact that the only anthracite or hard coal in the United States is located and was discovered in the North East section of Pennsylvania, basically running from Pottsville in the southern section known as Schulykill County and Carbon county up into Luzerne, Lackawanna and Wayne county. The first iron works were located in the Scranton area using the hard coal to make the iron and it was kept hidden the idea that soft coal can be used. Thereafter during the Industrial Revolution the need for steel created a demand for the use of coking coal (which was soft coal). Anthracite was tried in the early years in the

Scranton, Pennsylvania area and the first iron operations were in the Scranton area and from those operations subsequently was created the Bethlehem Steel Corporation which also was funded by those people in the anthracite regions that had the land and coal rights and the risk money. As we go forward into the Industrial Revolution these same practices continued up to 1900.

A new circumstance developed in 1901 when oil was discovered in Texas by a driller (wild catter)who pumped the oil out of the ground creating a new form of fuel. This signaled the beginning of the end for the anthracite industry. Along with the discovery and use of natural gas there was created a situation where the usage of oil which had been taking place from the early 1850's for other uses than fuel now erupted into fuel usage and the natural gas was now seen as a substitute for the hard coal and low BTU gas. Manufactured gas from hard coal had expanded all over the eastern U. S. and therefore the necessary pipelines were already in place in the eastern parts of the U. S.

After 1901, came the beginning of the demise of the so called anthracite coal industry. In 1920 at the peak of anthracite production Luzerne County in North Eastern Pennsylvania mined more than 120 million tons of anthracite coal a year resulting in 60 million in the coffers of the North East Pennsylvania land owner trusts through royalties. These royalties came from agreements that were arranged by those Connecticut Yankees who purchased the ground after the earlier stated grant dispute. Therefore there was a tremendous amount of cash (because of no income tax up to the point of 1930) placed into the trusts of the landowners. This cash hoard resulted from a 25 to 50 cents per ton royalty on each ton of coal mined from each coal vein. At that time coal was selling for $2.00 a ton retail or $2.50 and at most $5.50 per ton. As a side line, to indicate the accumulation of wealth at that time in the economy of the entire United States there were 200 to 300 millionaires. More than 200 of these millionaires were located in North Eastern Pennsylvania either delineated as individuals or hidden as trust participants.

In succeeding chapters we will go into the discovery of anthracite's early roles, how anthracite coal industry led up to Introduction of Rail lines throughout the North East and the rest of the country in order to bring the coal to market. We will review the power and influence of those who were receiving the coal royalties which led to the creation of new industry in the Industrial Revolution. We will go into the demise of the anthracite industry and the lessening of anthracite production brought about by the increase in oil, soft coal and natural gas industries.

Throughout 130 years until 1930 most of the economy and politics of the United States were controlled and directed by the large amounts of royalty money from anthracite coal coming into the economy directly and indirectly. The amount of cash money in trusts was so large that there had to be a way to utilize this money instead of just letting it lay dormant. It is well known that the income tax law's did not come into being until 1930 and as a matter of fact no one really paid any income tax until near 1940 and this was in the 1 or 2% range. So all of this money for 130 years until 1930 was essentially tax free and could be invested in business 100%. It was therefore useable money for investment in any business or other venture. I will relate how the use of this money through the various people came to give rise to quite a few well known industries which until now it had not been known that those industries were actually funded by and the beginnings of them came about because of trust moneys derived from the anthracite coal industry. Further ,I will try to show that in the early part of the 19th century as oil was discovered in Texas and Oklahoma ,which states were not controlled by Pennsylvania coal powers, the hand writing was on the wall for the demise of the anthracite coal industry. However ,the soft coal that was now being developed also gave rise to the increase in the steel industry in World War I. By that time the peak of anthracite production had been reached around 1920 when in Wyoming Valley in North East Pennsylvania more than 120 million tons of coal per year were being produced thus resulting in available cash in the coal trusts of

60 million dollars (in today's dollars 1.2 billion) from the Wyoming Valley Luzerne County area.

From 1920 on anthracite coal production declined and was given up by the coal interests and parceled off to other people who took the leavings. These people would continue to mine the coal, however, the competition from soft coal, oil, and natural gas had already begun to eat into the areas where anthracite had previously been the dependent key factor for home heating and industry. Therefore, there was a loss of profit to these new interests however the royalties of .50 per ton continued to be paid into the coal trusts. This resulted in lesser capital going into the trusts and now there was a bite from United States Government in the form of Income Tax. The coal interests income began to waiver from the use of anthracite but already previous wise investments through the house of Morgan (a connection we will discuss later) continued to reap benefits for the trusts. There was still quite a bit of production of anthracite even into the 40's and 50's ,however ,the uses were different and competition took its toll on the profit potential and yield to the trusts (SEE FIG.6)

In the 1960's the anthracite coal industry was for all practical purposes dead. With the demise of the anthracite industry, the North Eastern Pennsylvania was changed by necessity from a coal mining industry to a diversified type of industry. We will show in future chapters how the actual demise of the industry affected the population in North Eastern Pennsylvania both psychologically, physically, and economically,. creating in the people and subsequent generations even through 1999 a lack of self-esteem and a feeling of inferiority. This continues in 1999 even though anthracite coal production in the 1960's was dead for all practical purposes.

It is sketchy as to whether any actual claim of the Connecticut people had rights beyond what is now known as the Penn-Ohio border. However within this border of Pennsylvania there lay bountiful riches. The area contained vast amounts of timber, anthracite coal, and soft coal, oil, and natural gas. As we go further into the discovery and use of the anthracite coal, we will show how the other items played an important role in controlling the economy of the U. S.

In the late 1700's one of the early settlers was out in the woods and noticed this brown material coming up out of the ground and he took some of it back to his home and touched a match to tinder under it and found out that the material burned. So he went back and took more of the material and began to use it within the fireplaces where the homes were at that time were fueled by wood. The actual discovery that this brown and black material could burn in a fireplace in an open grate was later done by Judge Jesse Fell in the Fell house in Wilkes-Barre city.

Once it was discovered that the brown material, which was actually what was called the out crop of the anthracite, could burn, they dug down deeper and found the material became black and hard as crystal, becoming harder and harder as they dug further into the ground. This harder material tended to burn longer and give off more heat. As the material got harder and blacker it actually came from the deeper ground. It was really the better coal because it burned cleaner and gave off more heat or BTU's. Since this coal material was discovered and was found to be much more durable and more heat producing than wood and found to be abundant in this area, The owners of the land began to explore the idea of utilizing the coal to protect themselves financially. They immediately set up a system by which the tonnage of material taken out from the ground was protected by what was called politically a mineral rights clause and any of the ground owned by the Connecticut Yankees was only sold off with the mineral rights protected for the owner .To further entrench themselves for the future, they set it up so that each deed of trust containing mineral that was extracted from each coal vein beneath the surface was to be paid for by the tonnage amount and the deeds were set up as either .25 or .50 a ton which at that time in the early 1800's, coal was being sold for 1.75 to 5.00/ton. The owners were receiving into the trust accounts the .50/ton and as the coal became more in demand the figure that was placed as a royalty was .50/ton of coal mined.

To further control the mining of coal it was determined that it would be advisable to set up a central controlling brokerage firm so that the control of the coal being sold could be done through a central house (Hollenback coal exchange) and this way the price of the coal could be controlled and royalty collected honestly and correctly since this was the only source of anthracite coal in the U. S. This also was in the latitude grant location of the land primarily owned or controlled by the Connecticut charter co. and their descendants and friends. The pioneers who settled the area were well known and have been detailed in other works but for the sake of clarity some of the names will be repeated at times for particular emphasis and the signers of the oak tree charter will be referred as those of the Susquehanna Co. .It can be seen as time went by, the succeeding generations of these people and the monies derived from the coal either by direct profit from sale of the coal or by royalty were to be protected by English Trusts. They were American trusts but modeled after English trusts and some were actually set up in England. These trusts exist to this day and principally they were designed to control the outflow of the coal money so it could not be squandered by future generations of the coal landowners. These were not set up initially as so called interlocking trusts to the extent that they would violate laws (now known as antitrust laws), but when push came to shove the trust members who were in control of the various trusts (who were lawyers self taught in most part but also relatives of the trust members) could get together to vote when their interests were threatened. Further they naturally knew one another and without polling would vote in certain matters to keep the status quo or change it as each business case demanded.

In 1662 King Charles granted to Connecticut the upper half of Pennsylvania then King Charles in 1681 granted to William Penn a charter for the same land in the new world called America which was later to be known as Pennsylvania, after the granting of the charters it was determined the charter granted earlier to Connecticut was conflicting with the charter granted to William Penn in 1681. Incidentally Connecticut was the only colony of the thirteen colonies ever set up as a profit making venture. All of the other colonies were granted for various reasons by the King of England to various people and not necessarily to be known as profit making operations.

Significantly it was discovered by the Connecticut people that their charter ran conflicting with the Pennsylvania charter from a latitude bordering the southern part of New York (now known as New York) and the middle section of Pennsylvania north of Allentown and the middle of Ohio running all the way to the Mississippi. The grant was actually worded in such a manner that the grant to the Connecticut colony was stated that the grant was good in those longitudinal sections from the Atlantic Ocean all the way to the next great water. From ocean to ocean (SEE FIG.28) and at that time is was not known that the Pacific Ocean was there so the Connecticut people as they made their survey determined that the Mississippi was the great water and so actually they ended or did not pursue their claim beyond Mississippi for the above and other good reasons.

Later after the two Pennamite wars, sometimes called the first Civil War, the matter was settled in the courts (with regard to the Pennsylvania grant). The judge settled this case by confirming that the land was purchased by the Connecticut Yankees from the Indians for five thousand dollars and therefore was given to the Connecticut settlers (SEE FIG.3) as legitimate land owners.

The land however was slated and directed to be named Pennsylvania because of the William Penn Grant. Many people even today do not realize that one half of Pennsylvania was at one time owned and claimed by the Colony of Connecticut. The people did not realize that one half of Pennsylvania was owned by Connecticut People and as made known earlier, the Connecticut Colony was (a profit making type of corporation). There were certain people (the Susquehanna company) who had those particular land rights and the first settlement in North East Pennsylvania in 1769 came to be known as the Westmoreland County of Connecticut.

This land by coincidence encompassed all of the known anthracite or hard coal in America. In the 1790's the coal was discovered as an out crop or surface coal vein which was brown in color and resembled vegetation. When the settlers first picked up the particles they found that the particles actually could burn. Later Judge Jesse Fell in what was known as the Fell House in the City of Wilkes-Barre (SEE FIG 16) first burned anthracite coal on an open grate. This opened the door to coal as a substitute for wood burning in fireplaces and other uses since the coal burned longer and gave off more heat than wood. This led to anthracite coal as a home heating fuel and further in iron and steel making .furthermore it led to the use of anthracite in locomotives (instead of wood) and then further in the production of low BTU gas all of this taking place before natural gas and oil were discovered or marketed from Western Pennsylvania or other locations in the U.S. such as Texas and Oklahoma . Later, in Western Pennsylvania oil and gas were uncovered and allowed to be produced for fuel.

Due to the fact that coal, was already so greatly used, the canals in the 1820's and '30's were overwhelmed and the Connecticut settlers who owned the ground and coal rights went to certain people to create rail systems to carry the coal to markets in the northeast and then to the Midwest of the United States. The trains would carry the black gold to the various markets. Subsequently the coal was then used in factories to create steam and drive various machines by means of pulley belts thus beginning the Industrial Revolution.

The usage of the hard coal was increased voluminously, because as was stated before, there was no discovery of the soft coal in the western Pennsylvania areas since the people from Connecticut who owned these land rights all the way to the Mississippi did not call for such action.

CHAPTER 2

❊

Expanding The Power Base

In the early 1800's, (1801 to 1838) after the discovery of the anthracite coal and the various uses that the coal might be put to, Connecticut being a profit making corporation, it was determined that they would expand the coal usage as much as possible while keeping hidden through their control the ground containing the soft coal, gas, and oil contained in their land rights in Western Pennsylvania and through Ohio.

It was already demonstrated that hard coal was much more efficient than wood and the demand skyrocketed for more of the black gold by the burgeoning population in the new world and for the ever increasing expansion to the west. So from 1801 to 1838 the demand was so great for coal that the canals (built through their political influence with the state government of Pennsylvania) to move the coal on barges was overloaded. Mine after mine, was opened and obviously these were not coal mines that were opened principally by the original owner of the ground but by their friends or acquaintances or those upon whom they would place their trust and shower the opportunity on them , by providing the capital to open the mines. Principally, these were friends or relatives or friends of friends but they were also capable business men. The idea being, that it would be more or less that the prosperity from the coal proceeds would be kept in the family or a close circle of trusted people.

In the early 1800's there was a great need for the technical skill to extract the coal from the ground. The expertise that was needed was available from England. Once the Connecticut Yankees realized this they brought over the Welsh from Wales who already had the skills of opening new mines and mining coal in Wales and could be counted upon to do good work and be faithful servants. The high English who were primarily Presbyterian and Episcopalian and were the owners of the ground then used their connections to begin bringing Welsh people over into North East Pennsylvania, with the idea of having the Welsh to be the mine worker not owners. This was principally the bulk of the people who came to North Eastern Pennsylvania in the early 1800's.

Later the Irish would come over to work in the coal mines and they could fit in well with the Welsh miners with both speaking the same language and also needing work and not looking at all for a business opportunity. This system of having the welsh and Irish work together allowed for good communication between owners and workers, since all spoke the English language. It should be mentioned now that the people who set the whole system up of extracting coal from the mines etc. were rather brilliant business people.

In the 1800's (it's difficult to actually piece together), because of the lack of information, and the fact that many of these agreements between the owners , who came from Connecticut, and many of the trusts were hidden. Therefore, it is by studying what actually happened and who actually appeared and what came about, that we know the background. For example, the coal became great in demand and was so plentiful that there was no way to get it to market conveniently as there were no rail roads and there was no waterway that could efficiently transport the coal to market.

The Bureau of Mines was not created until 1903 and actual state government overlook of mine operations (pitiful as it may be) did not occur until 1870 and beyond. Since there was such a great demand at the early stage of the beginning of the Industrial Revolution there were some brilliant people who devised a method of canals that stretched from New York to the Chesapeake Bay and it was along those canals and down into Philadelphia along the Delaware river that the barge system transported the coal to market. Delivery of the coal was set up along the canal route where drop off brokers were arranged ,all in the control of the North Eastern Pennsylvania coal producers and landowners. This allowed the people who would purchase coal to pick the coal up at a convenient stop, but the Connecticut people still maintained control.

Here again in the early 1800's as the first mines began to appear they copied the mines in Wales where coal was being produced by the Welsh so that each Colliery (maybe a little differently than what is in Wales) was set up as an actual small town with it's own stores, churches, homes, etc. and interspersed there were dry goods and other stores, restaurants, and beer taverns. So that each colliery was in effect set up as a small town.

Since there were agreements for royalties by owners of the ground and minerals it was sort of an unwritten law that if one colliery(town) was set up then the next colliery given to someone to develop (there were written and unwritten conditions) would not steal (for example) workers from each other. There was in essence one owner family of all the ground and the landowners did not want the people who they gave the rights to mine coal to be fighting among themselves for workers. So they kept the workers within that confine or colliery and more or less each town developed along this sort of line. This strategy was not known to the people who were in the town mining the coal and they were not aware that they were being manipulated in such a manner for the benefit of the coal and land owners.

More or less the collieries were set up in the way of the old English feudal system where (for example) the king had his castle and a moat around it such as the colliery confines with the stores and the church and supply house all built around it similar to the feudal serfs farming the ground around the king's castle and therefore they were beholden to the lord and master. They would give a share of their goods to the lord and master.

In order to make those people more subservient to that dogma, the area of the due bill was introduced. This was a situation where the mine owner in order to protect his cadre of men would have them (since they owned the stores, the houses, the land, in essence all) deduct from the person working at the end of the week his rent, his supplies, his store bill, and whatever else was owed and the net amount would be the pay in cash money or script that the miners or laborers would take home to his family if in fact there were any thing due to the coal miner. So you can see that nowhere in the United States, at least even in the settlement of the west ,was there anything comparable to this kind of set up except there might have been some vestige of that copied later in the iron mining operations out west, where the company set up all the facilities for the people. Though that was not the same kind of a thing because the iron mining operations while they were extensive, the iron mining people did not own all of the ground in the areas where they were mining the ore, they only owned a portion of the ground, and in other cases they only leased the ground, so it was not comparable to the coal mining situation in North Eastern Pennsylvania. To my mind there was not a comparable area in the United States or even possibly the world that was quite similar to this business set up in North Eastern Pennsylvania. I would stand corrected if there is another situation where a business corporation owned the ground, the mineral rights and basically owned the people within the confines by virtue of a system that was put in place to extract the anthracite coal.

In order to continue this, another brilliant strategy developed in the early 1800's. Since these people owned all of the ground all the way out to Western Pennsylvania and through Ohio and to the Mississippi, there was knowledge by the land owners that there existed soft coal and oil and gas in Western Pennsylvania and Ohio. In order to protect this bounty of hard coal in North East Pennsylvania and utilize it to its maximum with their shrewd business sense. They deliberately declined to mine the soft coal or to exploit the gas and oil in the ground they owned in Western Pennsylvania. They did this by controlling the money supply which would be necessary to go forward in exploiting these other resources.

Later this was accomplished, but for 100 years until oil was discovered by a wild cat oil driller in Texas, in 1901 they prospered with the hard coal royalties and the hidden bounty in Western Pennsylvania and Ohio remained hidden. They never perceived a significant threat to their dominance. In fact as we point out later their control of the political system and by utilizing the shrewdness and brilliance of J. P. Morgan and their money, they controlled the United States economy and it's politics. The coal then became the dominant fuel produced for the United States even to the extent of Providing low BTU gas from coal to provide gas lights and later production furnaces during the Industrial Revolution. This gas was produced by burning coal and then passing steam through the burning coals to produce a low BTU gas. By compressing the gas they could send it through pipelines where it could be utilized for various purposes but deliberately not for heating until after 1940- and beyond. To this day 1999 most of gas supply lines are in the east and the north of the United States. The existing pipelines of today that transport natural gas through cities in the east are the result of this early venture into low BTU gas. This groundwork was laid by the people who I will name in a later chapter.

People who came early to the North Eastern Pennsylvania were mainly the Welsh and the Irish. This gave them a feeling of being serfs or commonly known today as slaves, although these people who were brought here to work the coal mines never felt in their hearts and minds that they were slaves, because to them the new world (with a job) was an opportunity for them that did not exist from whence they came. They came from Wales where getting low wages, serfdom and impoverishment to higher wages and opportunity here in North Eastern Pennsylvania. The same held true with the Irish as they also were experiencing hard times in Ireland except that the Irish when they came to mine the coal were not given the better jobs for obvious reasons, even though they spoke the same language. This persisted in the early years of Irish immigration and even into the late 1800's. So that the immigrants until approximately 1840 when the canals were unable to handle all the coal were primarily Welsh.

We will attempt to segregate distinct periods of time to show how the influence of market control affected immigration into the United States and North Eastern Pennsylvania. We have to look at the area from 1800 to 1838 when the canals were overloaded. It is very difficult in researching to establish the exact shakers and movers since there were economic decisions among people of power and done in private secret meeting not subject to the same rules we see in business today. For example, The Sherman Antitrust Act did not become enforced until the 1930's and beyond event though enacted in 1870's and held in check by the coal interests through their power and influence of their steward J. P. Morgan. They even elected 7 presidents from Ohio with the control derived from the anthracite coal funds and political expertise of their bag man Mark Hanna of Ohio who was funded with a coal mine given to him in North East Pennsylvania to provide some of the money to accomplish this political purpose.

CHAPTER 3

Anthracite Coal Production Increases, Profits Increase, and A Financial Genius Appears

J. P. Morgan magnified the connections his father had with the coal trusts in North Eastern Pennsylvania J. P. Morgan was born in 1837 in Hartford Connecticut of wealthy parents. His father Junius Morgan had already started the Morgan Bank in New York City and was connected to the Susquehanna Co. and Hartford which owned all of North Eastern Pennsylvania lands, as was stated previously. While J. P. Morgan was growing up his father was involved with the coal interests in North Eastern Pennsylvania through the Connecticut and Philadelphia connections. This enabled the railroads to come into North Eastern Pennsylvania by way of a franchise to Asa Packer after 1840. In addition deals had been struck with Morgan and the New York Bank to make investments from coal proceeds in the gold and silver mines in the west taking back to the east at least 150 million in profits. In 1858 the North East people contracted to construct the transcontinental (Union

Pacific) railroad beginning in Bethlehem Pennsylvania feigning a cooperative effort with their San Francisco stooges to make the trans continental railroad more palatable to the politicians who were against it and to hide the monopoly. These same people from northeast Pennsylvania organized the Bethlehem Steel corporation.

At the age of 21 young J. P. Morgan went into the Morgan bank and after taking over the operation changed the name of the bank to J. P. Morgan Bank & Trust Co. His father Junius was in London funneling coal money to the U.S. from the coal trusts. Young J.P. morgan magnified the connections his father had with the coal trusts in n.e. pennsylvania as he began to see the opportunity for use of their capital in promoting his schrewd business decisions he began to see the opportunity for use of their capital in promoting his shrewd business decisions.

He began his career as a great manipulator of investment capital. In 1890 even though the Sherman Antitrust Act was previously passed ,Sherman and others did not implement it. It was left to Teddy Roosevelt to try to begin to feign the act. Morgan had kept it bottled up until that time through his political protective connections. He then arranged the oil trust (which provided the greases and lubricant for the coal mines in North East Pennsylvania) by using the acumen of a mere penniless accountant named John D. Rockefeller .Then Morgan's bank having previously financed Andrew Carnegie put together 8 other steel companies with Carnegies homestead plant to form the United States Steel Company in 1901. Because the Bethlehem steel corporation was organized by North Eastern coal trust interests it was deliberately told to Morgan to keep his hands off and Bethlehem steel was left out of the United States steel corporation but was still financed through the Morgan Bank and North Eastern Pennsylvania coal trust interests and their coal trust money.

In his actions with Ted Roosevelt, even though Roosevelt appeared the reformer and antagonist of Morgan, Roosevelt had to call on

Morgan for help both in the Panama Canal deal and later the resolution of the bank panic of 1907 through the help of Ted's brother in law Douglas Robinson, who was a partner of J.P. Morgan. Even Roosevelt was not aware that all of Morgan's risk capital investment money was coming from North Eastern Pennsylvania coal royalties through the Morgan Partners from North East Pennsylvania and the coal trust money forwarded from England by his father Junius Morgan.

Having tired of Andrew Carnegie's lack of attention to the homestead steel and iron works which J. P. Morgan was financing ,Morgan decided that the time had come to finally get rid of Andrew Carnegie . Morgan having previously purchased several small steel companies knew he had to get rid of Carnegie to move his plans forward to create a massive steel conglomerate to be known as the United States steel corporation

An interesting sideline to the Andrew Carnegie story is that when J. P. Morgan decided to form the United States Steel corporation and needed to buy out Andrew Carnegie Homestead Steel Works, he sent a messenger to ask Carnegie how much money he wanted for the Homestead Works. The reply was 480 million(requested by Carnegie)and at the time a fabulous amount. J. P. never hesitated and told his man to tell Carnegie it was a deal. Upon the conclusion J. P. told Carnegie he was the richest man in the world, never letting Carnegie know that Morgan had fooled him by setting the payment terms, which were 300 million of paper (potentially worthless) bonds in his various ventures which were only paper as valued by Morgan, and 180 million in cash currency. To this day until revealed here, Carnegie thought he got the better of the deal but Morgan outfoxed him with 300 million of paper which could have been worthless. As it turned out Morgan's ventures, due to absolute monopolies, were all virtually successful and thereby resulted inadvertently in a windfall for Carnegie. Carnegie died never realizing he had been made a fool of by J. Peirpoint Morgan and through luck Carnegie had recovered financially due to the company bonds being redeemed at the face value and better.

19

Another reason, not brought out before ,why Morgan demanded that Carnegie sell out was that Morgan was financing Carnegie's Homestead steel works with North east Pennsylvania coal trust money and his stooge who was at the Homestead Works reported that Carnegie was spending too much time in Scotland and not enough paying attention to the problems in Homestead, particularly the strike when Carnegie was in Scotland.

Morgan was one of the world's foremost financial figures in the decades before World War I. He organized railroads at the behest of the coal trust people and formed the United States Steel Corporation as mentioned before. His apparent wealth and financial management skills were so considerable that he was able to steer the Unites States Treasury from the brink of financial disaster. J. P. Morgan was born in Hartford Connecticut on April 17 1837 his father was a very successful businessman, and John Peirpoint was educated at Germany's distinguished University of Gottingen. In 1871 he became a partner in the New York City firm of Drexel, Morgan and Company. In 1895 the firm was renamed J. P. Morgan and Company and it soon grew to be one of the most powerful banking houses. Morgan had a talent with North East coal trust money for merging and reorganizing struggling companies to make them remarkably profitable. He always tried to have two players competing against each other.

In 1885 he began a long career in railroad organization when he arranged for the merger of the New York Central Rail Road with competing New York lines. Within three years he extended his influence ,due to urging by North East Pennsylvania trust interests, to railways based in Pennsylvania and Ohio. After a financial panic in 1893 he helped to rehabilitate a number of major lines and stabilize the railroad industry by reducing competition. A good example of this is when he forced the abandonment of the Southern Pennsylvania route which was conveniently bailed out later to become the first

Pennsylvania turnpike When Morgan arranged these mergers he also became a stockholder in the railroad companies and by 1900 he was one of the world's most influential railroad leaders even though no one knew that the actual owners were North East Pennsylvania coal land owners and mine owners.

In the winter of 1895 when the United States Treasury was on the verge of bankruptcy, Morgan organized a group of financiers from North Eastern Pennsylvania who carried out a private bond sale to replenish the treasury. He helped the government again in 1907 when, with Wall Street in a financial crisis, Morgan used his control of the banking houses to take government deposits.

In 1898 Morgan formed the Federal Steel Company and in 1901 he united it with the homestead works and various other steel companies to form the vast United States Steel Corporation. He also financed International Harvester and the International Merchant Marine and at least 112 other major U. S. companies. Morgan was not praised for such financial wizardry and in 1912 a federal committee investigated his operations. It was thought by the government and others at the time that his consolidation of companies created unfair monopolies.

In the final report of the Pujo Committee it was shown that Morgan (the dictator) and his partners indeed controlled all of the major industries in the United States. It was never really determined by the committee that Morgan had a money trust. Indeed he did have a money trust as revealed in this book but the Congressional committee could not determine that a money trust existed or that it was from the North East Pennsylvania coal royalties. For reference the final report of the Pujo Committee (SEE FIG 1) and a biography of Pujo (SEE FIG 23)are attached. This information clearly shows the power that Morgan and his partners had to control the entire financial dealings in the U. S. including the ability to bail out the U.S. Treasury. While escaping any criminal indictments, Morgan due to the extreme pressure of these hearings by the Pujo Committee passed away in 1913.

French Asylum

Located on a broad stretch of land next to a horseshoe bend in the Susquehanna River lies a community built for Queen Marie Antoinette. French immigrants traveled to Philadelphia then traveled overland to Wilkes-Barre where they bought boats and supplies from Matthias Hollenback. They traveled up river to what is now known as Wyalusing there to build the community which lasted from 1793 to 1803 and known as French Azilum. In 1797 visitors from France traveled to Azilum and on return stayed as a guest in Wilkes-Barre at David Hayfield Conyngham's home who was the family agent of a shipping firm and ancestor to John N. Conyngham II (partner of J. P. Morgan) who built hayfield house in the Wyoming Valley. The original asylum was thought to be financed by Robert Morris who was purported to be the financier of the American Revolution. However, it is now known that the Conyngham family ancestors gave the money to Robert Morris to give to George Washington.

Jesse Fell Coal Pioneer

Luzerne County's first mayor changed more than the political climate in his day—he revolutionized the way a nation heated itself. Jesse Fell—Quaker, innkeeper, sheriff, mayor and judge(SEE FIG 16)—made a lasting impact with his innovative use of anthracite coal in 1808. Early valley residents used the "hard" coal found in the area as a heat source, but couldn't keep it burning without a consistent draft. Fell discovered that smaller chunks of coal burned longer on an open grate. New coal could be placed on the fire and the ashes would fall down, creating a constant heat source that was reliable and economical. Soon others in the area took advantage of the easily available anthracite coal. Fell's simple idea played a major role in the growing industrialization of the new nation. The anthracite coal so abundant in the Wyoming Valley provided a safe and inexpensive form of energy to fuel the railroads and machines throughout the country. Fell held various political offices in Luzerne County, including clerk of courts and associate judge of Luzerne County Courts, a position he held for 32 years. The old Fell house where Jesse Fell made his discovery was built in 1787 and rebuilt in 1905. The house stood at the corner of East Northampton and Washington Streets in Wilkes-Barre until its demolition. For many years it was Luzerne County's oldest licenses hotel.

General John Sullivan Road Designer

Wyoming Valley's first planned thoroughfare wasn't designed for venture but rather for vengeance. The lower road to Delaware, as it was known in the 18th century, was surveyed and redesigned by General John "Black Jack" Sullivan in 1779 to accommodate his troops in a bloody trail of destruction of the Iroquois Indians. Originally an attorney from New Hampshire, Sullivan served in the Continental Army and was commissioned by General George Washington to punish the Indians for the Wyoming Massacre and remove threat of future attacks. Sullivan built up the Lower Road, gathered supplies and finally led an army of 3,500 men up the trail from Easton to Wilkes-Barre and up to the Genessee River in upstate New York. Following Washington's orders, Sullivan destroyed 40 Indian settlements and 160,000 bushels of corn. He returned to Wilkes-Barre after pushing the Iroquois beyond the Niagara. Sullivan later retired from the army and served as New Hampshire's Attorney General. In 1788, he was presiding officer of the New Hampshire contingent that approved the U. S. Constitution. Sullivan's mark on the Wyoming Valley can still be seen today. Northampton street from South River street in Wilkes-Barre to Laurel Run closely follows the Sullivan Trail. It also was known as the Easton and Wilkes-Barre Turnpike and once served as the main toll road in and out of the Wyoming Valley.

A thumbnail description of the anthracite coal area in Northeast Pennsylvania The upper Susquehanna—Lackawanna watershed, designated by the United States Environmental Protection Agency and the U.S. Geological Survey comprise nearly 1,800 square miles of land and almost 1,600 miles of perennial rivers and streams. This area contains major urban centers including Wilkes-Barre and Scranton cities. In 1990 640,000 people lived in the region and it is the third largest metropolitan area in Pennsylvania.

It is supposed that 300+ million years ago a shallow sea covered the watershed of the Wyoming valley and Lackawanna County areas depositing fine grained sediments producing sandstone and shale. Prehistoric swamp also covered the area for long periods of time. The trees and other vegetation were compressed and formed large deposits of anthracite coal. This coal was formed by great pressures and resulted in the only place in the United States where anthracite coal was found. The hardest anthracite coal was found in deep mines called (veins) and the hardest coal was found in Luzerne and Lackawanna Counties. Additionally, anthracite coal was found in Schykill, Carbon, and Wayne Counties but was not of the hardness and quality of coal found in Luzerne and Lackawanna County. It is supposed that the glaciers put such tremendous pressure on the land that this resulted in the vegetation turning to hard coal.

Morgan devil, saint, tyrant, philanthropist, financier. Not one of these but a combination of all. No one who felt the wrath of Morgan would call him anything but a financial devil. In his rescue of the U.S. Government from a number of financial panics you would think he was a saint protectors. As an art collector and donator of various art works including the Morgan Library his philanthropy emerged. But his greatest role and one for which he overshadows both his father and son is that of his ability to bow to the wishes of the coal trust in northeast

Pennsylvania by establishing industry everywhere in the U.S. except in the North East Pennsylvania coal region. He knew he had to obey the coal trust orders to get the risk capital he needed to finance and control his other business ventures. If he had no risk capital he could go nowhere financially. He had to bow to the coal trust representatives and not make a mistake and lose their risk capital. Further he dared not interfere in their operations in North East Pennsylvania except when asked. Why didn't Morgan include Bethlehem Steel in the U.S. Steel Plan? The reason is simple, had he interfered in Bethlehem steel which was organized by the coal trust interests his flow of risk capital would dry up. He knew as all great people know their limitations. His organization of railroads stopped at the North East Pennsylvania corridor. That territory belonged to Asa Packer and the coal trust interests. As a consolation his Pennsylvania and Reading Railroad was given the Schuylkill mines a collection of 100 mines in which to run the rails. But the Pottsville area while rich in coal was not as good a coal as that in Luzerne and Lackawanna Counties. The coal trust interests gave him the rights to trouble and the home of the Irish Molly MaGuires who were the first union organizers in the United States business history. Morgan through his stooge who he had running the Pennsylvania and reading railroad trumped up charges against Black Jack Kehoe and fixed the trial to have him hanged. Black Jack was later exonerated by the Governor of Pennsylvania Milton Shapp.

William Gildersleeve Abolitionist

If the child is the father of the man, the young William Camp Gildersleeve must have been profoundly disturbed at the sight of slaves being sold in front of his preacher father's church in Georgia. For when he reached adulthood, Gildersleeve, a 19th -century abolitionist, moved to Wilkes-Barre and helped runaway slaves escape the south via the so-called underground railroad.

Gildersleeve would hide runaway slaves in his kitchen, then shuttle them to Scranton. Eventually, they would reach slave-free Canada. Prosecuted by a slave owner, he once told a Philadelphia court: "I plead guilty to having helped runaway slaves get to Canada. I felt I was obeying a higher law, even, than my country's."

Though the U.S. census (even the United States government was ignorant of the slave conditions in the coal mines in northeast Pennsylvania) showed no slave owners in the Wyoming Valley in 1821, the year Gildersleeve moved here, there was little support for his anti-slave cause. The slaves were already here as white slaves in the coal mines of North East Pennsylvania. In 1837, Gildersleeve invited a prominent abolitionist to the community to deliver an anti-slave oratory. When area churches and politicians refused to give the abolitionist a place to speak, Gildersleeve let him use his 50-acre estate on South Main Street, between South and Ross Streets. A waiting mob vandalized Gildersleeve's home. Two years later, another anti-slave speech was delivered at his home. This time, the mob grabbed Gildersleeve, soaked him with black dye and paraded him through the city which now has a street named for him.

Isn't it ironic that Gildersleeve tried to free the slaves in the south never realizing he was in the midst of coal mine slaves.

CHAPTER 4

The Period 1840 to 1870—Anthracite Coal and the Second Civil War

Now in 1838 and 1840 it became apparent that the canals that were built with help from the political interests of Pennsylvania at the state level could not handle the demands for transporting anthracite coal to market. Since coal was so superior to wood for the purposes of heat and for other purposes,. uses for coal magnified and what took place was the demand for the hard coal became so great, just for heating alone, that the canals could not carry all of the coal to market. These coal trust people of North East Pennsylvania of great business acumen and economic foresight and great intelligence and great fortitude saw the handwriting on the wall. They knew that they needed some other form of mass transportation for the anthracite coal. Cars were not in existence, trucks were not in existence, the horse and buggy couldn't haul the coal, but the water they thought could, but the water canals were overwhelmed so what were they to do? They took the capital that was available from the coal trust royalties and took the money from their banks that they had control of and they brought in Asa Packer to build the rail systems in North East Pennsylvania to serve each of the coal collieries. Nobody would have known that Asa Packer would be chosen to do the job of bringing in all the rails into North Eastern Pennsylvania to move the coal out, but he was given free reign by those in power in northeast Pennsylvania to do just that, To bring in the rails and so he did. He put rails all over the coal producing areas. Now the franchise was given to Asa Packer to bring in the rails to the collieries in North East Pennsylvania (they could never get away with it today because of the anti-trust laws). The franchise was given to Asa Packer and to Asa Packer alone and as they saw that they maybe needed extra help they gave the rail franchise to others such as the Pennsylvania Railroad and secretly to J. P. Morgan, but Asa Packer got the best rights, the easy rights and the correct rights. He got what was necessary (a blank check) from the coal trusts to bring in the rails and so he did bring in the rails where they told him to bring the rails. To the various collieries in North East Pennsylvania so that they could take the coal out and that coal tonnage aside from bringing a profit to the mine owners and their heirs also brought a royalty and so it would behoove them to move the coal out as quick as possible because it was in such demand by the rest of the country. They opened up the banks to Asa Packer and he put the rail roads in all the way up to Southern New York so that he could connect onto whatever other rail roads were set up by the Morgan people that were available like the Central Rail Road in New York and such as the New Jersey central Rail Road and then the coal trust people also set up another rail road that they would control the Union Pacific out of Bethlehem and they later set up the Bethlehem Steel Corporation . But in order to bring in the rail roads they needed someone like Asa Packer who would do their bidding make ,a profit doing it ,and who was capable and knowledgeable enough to know how to do the job and get it done correctly and quickly. Obviously you would ask, why did they chose Asa Packer to do this job ?And the answer is, I don't know, and I don't know anyone who could tell me actually definitively why Asa Packer was chosen, but he was capable of doing the job and he did the job, bringing the rail roads to North East Pennsylvania. The Central Rail Road of New Jersey came in once Asa Packer had received his right aways and they put the rails in selected locations and then they could bring in anyone else they wanted to at their bidding and I emphasize at their bidding because as you know there were no antitrust laws in those days of 1840-1870 the civil war era. There were still no antitrust laws in effect and so there was no one who was going to question what money could do, what power it could wield and what collusive and political actions could be taken to benefit the movement of the hard coal. Rail roads were brought in (canals went down the drain) they were practically useless and were abandoned once the rail roads were put in and so the coal moved by rail. Hundreds of cars, thousands of cars ending up with millions of cars of coal to fuel the economy, the burgeoning and expanding economy of the United States.

In this next thirty year period there was an economic expansion that in the U.S. was unbelievable. With everything that took place in those next thirty years nothing in the last hundred fifty years could compare to it in North Eastern Pennsylvania. Now the economic progress, if you take what happened in North Eastern Pennsylvania with the construction of the rail roads, the coal production increasing (which again we will show whatever figures we have available for the coal production from 1840-1870 (SEE FIG 6) and we will show if we can those figures and what the economy of the United States (SEE FIG 8) was doing at that time. We can guesstimate from certain sources and we can also show what bank deposits were and what the treasury of the United States was at that time. We do know one thing ,we can estimate it by royalty figures., We can estimate the value of the owners trusts from whatever source we can gather figures (TOTAL ALL OF THE TONNAGE AND APPLY THE ROYALTY FIGURE) but again there is no way to document it from proof and I doubt that people who control and own the trusts ,even they would not have the figures to prove their case against what one might estimate. But it's important to put down these figures because it gives more credence to the statements that are being made as to the economic expansion, the usage of anthracite, and how the rail roads expanded and it shows that those figures will more or less indicate that this 1840-1870 was a great period of expansion.

Now in 1848 as you know there was a gold rush out in California and it's understood that a lot of currency that the hard coal mine owners had accumulated was utilized to invest in the gold mines in California and this the value of their investment multiplied quite drastically returning 150 to 170 million to the North East Pennsylvania coal trusts. Their assets multiplied because as you know there was a lot of gold and if those investments were wise and we have no knowledge as to what they actually did as far as multiplying their assets but these people were quite knowledgeable in business and economics and entrepreneurship it's only logical to assume the above. There is some evidence and there is some indication that this was done but we have no documented proof. We can only speculate as to how much was invested there but we know roughly how much came back in dividends. One thing we do know the money that went out to the west even then came from the east and the only great supply of money in the east was from the anthracite coal. profits and trusts.

Even up to 1960, in a study made by Governor Shapp of Pennsylvania, who at that time was working for John F. Kennedy, a study was made in one of the departments of commerce to determine where the money flowed in the United States . I happened to be at a seminar where Governor Shapp of Pennsylvania showed on a graph that most of the money in the east was being invested in the west so I would assume that if that was happening in 1960 that it also happened in 1848 when the gold rush was discovered because there was basically nothing out west, the west was hardly settled with any people. The banking system was poorly organized at that time the federal reserve banks had not come into play and the government treasury was not at all great. I would say that the money came from the only source of cash and that was from North Eastern Pennsylvania coal trusts.

In the period of 1840-1870 there was an influx of rail roads and a much greater movement of coal to the Philadelphia ,New York ,New Jersey area and out into whatever area was calling for coal for heat and then of course the rail roads began to burn the coal in the steam engines instead of wood and so that created a much greater demand again for coal. Of course in 1860 between 1850-1860 there was a great influx of rail roads and finalization of that and as you know in 1860 the second civil war came about and again there was a great demand for coal for the forging of weapons and for the materials and armor that was to carry out the civil war. Soft coal was still not being utilized to make iron or steel it was anthracite coal and wood that was being utilized and at that time so the best thing you can say about anthracite coal in that period of time is that there was a great expansion of production.

CHAPTER 5

The Industrial Revolution

Now what happened in North East Pennsylvania with the coal collieries, as the demand grew there was a need to open more collieries. Opening more collieries meant a demand for more labor and the demand for more labor meant that there had to be a decision made. That decision was (we need to get the labor) the shakers and the movers queried where do we get the labor and we have no proof as to what went through the minds of the movers and coal mine owners at that time. You have to remember one important thing and that is that they owned all the ground. They owned the underground, they owned the trees that grew on the upper ground, they owned the Western Pennsylvania with all the soft coal under it, the oil and the gas. They owned the only anthracite coal in the country and most importantly they lived here. The owners lived here where this coal production had to take place and they were not going to move out and be absentee owners. They were going to stay here and have their families here, make their homes here, have their children here and have their children's children live here. That was their thinking and so their thoughts came to mind ,who can we be most comfortable with. They already knew that they had brought in a number of Welsh of their own kind to work the mines. They had brought in the Irish and they began to bring in more of those but they ran into the resistance of more Irish coming over because they didn't want to leave the country. So they had to make a decision as to whether they were going to continue to try to talk more Welsh and Irish in to our area or are we going to have to look elsewhere and since we're going to live here, who do we want on our grounds and who would we feel most comfortable with. The thought came to mind, let's go and try to solicit people from Europe. Europe was a poor continent at the time jobs were not plentiful at all, so they sent paid agents over to Europe, to Russia, Poland, Czechoslovakia, Lithuania, Germany, France but for some reason they had very poor luck in France and Holland for people who would be willing to work in the coal mines but they had good luck with people in Poland, and Russia and Czechoslovakia and in Germany partly because they were used to hard work there and partly because there times there harder then the Dutch Netherlands and in France and so what happened was they sent agents and paid a bounty to solicit people to come over promising them a job, opportunity, a home and good pay. This was something that these people didn't have in their country so this is where they began to look for other workers. This would not come about until the next period of time that we are going to study but going back to the 1840-1870 period we now have the gold rush is over, the west is being settled, greater numbers of people are moving out for opportunity to the west, and there is an expanding economy in the east with a need for more energy. The rail roads now are going out into other areas of the country to move goods particularly the civil war goods. This began to burgeon the rail lines and so there was now a great transportation system to move the coal to the markets. To the places where it's needed and so there was a great expansion of coal production. We can show the steady rise of coal production how that relates to the income of the United States and how it affected some of the other things that went on. We'll mention some of the names again that will come into the forefront that we can verify to some extent who were the leaders in this effort to move this expansion forward both in our area and through correlation's and connections through other people who they felt could help them, in other areas of the country. In chapter VI 1870-1900 I'll show that some part of the Industrial Revolution began a few years before and that the greatest part of the Industrial Revolution in the United States took place in that thirty years, a remarkable expansion of the economy and guess what the biggest contributor to the Industrial Revolution both money wise and power wise was king coal. With the discovery of electricity by J. P. Morgan's man Thomas Edison there came a need for power generation and the only thing that could produce the power was the coal that was available in that period of time. So coal made the steam that drove the generators that produced electricity that also moved locomotives and moved machinery within manufacturing operations. About then came the discovery that there was a way of producing gas too from the coals and so low BTU gas was produced which brought about the necessity of pipelines. The pipes were produced from the steel which also used coal to make the steel and iron pipe so this was one thing multiplying another. From 1870-1900 you saw the greatest expansion of Industry and coal production and a great immigration from Europe and the great immigration came for two reasons one was to provide the labor to implement the Industrial Revolution in (which came about because of a 40% tariff put on imported goods through the influence of the presidents and others they elected) the United States and the other was to provide man power to mine the hard coal that was necessary to fuel the Industrial Revolution, to expand the people out to the west ,and provide them with all the necessities of life. Again we'll look at the statistics of what the estimate of the coal production was (SEE FIG 6) and what the gross national product was and what remained in the treasury of the coal trusts in North Eastern Pennsylvania due to the coal royalties. Now in some areas in 1870 in the United States there was a so called depression ,a slow down

,and that was due to the fact that the civil war was over and there was a calamity going about soldiers coming back that would need a job etc. and there was a reversal in the economy in the south the slaves were free now they would have to pay to employ them so there was confusion which caused a depression but the depression was short lived because the Industrial Revolution began to take hold and there was an upward spiral from then on so we'll look at all of the statistics and we'll try and give some scenario that the statistics create and explain what they mean and we'll try to mention who the shakers and movers were in this period of time in North Eastern Pennsylvania how they influenced and cooperated and collaborated with others in New York and Philadelphia areas which were the centers of commerce and the centers of banking and the centers of money.

Now another person that came about was Rockefeller and his rise in the 1850's and the late 1850's he was an accountant in Ohio. I said that Ohio was actually controlled by Pennsylvania and Connecticut and the upper part by the Connecticut Yankees. The money that was available was from North Eastern Pennsylvania and so it's my belief that since Rockefeller was an accountant that had no money then where did he get his money from to start buying all theses little oil companies? My belief is that he got it from the people in North Eastern Pennsylvania through J. P. Morgan and he made some deal with him and he invested to start buying these oil companies. He had the acumen and intelligence so Morgan backed him to do this job and I believe that Rockefeller got his start from the coal trust money through the house of Morgan either directly or indirectly he either got it directly from someone who he was partners with (silent partners) or got it from Morgan the bank which were fed the money from North Eastern Pennsylvania coal trusts. In that same period of time there was a bally who about antitrust laws and this was brought about by the excesses of Rockefeller and acquiring and controlling all these oil companies ,we'll show how this also impinged on activities of the coal trusts later.

1900-1920 now that period of time was the greatest period of pro-duction of anthracite coal, however in 1901 oil was discovered in Texas and this was the hand writing on the wall for the coal barons as they realized that while they had kept the oil in Western Pennsylvania hidden to some extent from expanding by controlling Rockefeller and con-trolled the ground where in it lay and since they as I mentioned had control of Rockefeller they could keep track of him to a certain extent until he later became more independent and got out of hand and became somewhat independent.

In 1901 when oil was discovered in Texas, because with the discovery of oil in Texas ,and the myriad of uses that were going to be imple-mented from oil then the hand writing was on the wall for the demise of the anthracite industry ,but it took 30+ years 1901-1930. And in that period of time the oil usage began to grow and the coal usage was still growing because there was still a tremendous demand and that was a period of world war 1.So there was a great demand for coal but then the oil was also becoming in demand because of the usage of car and trucks.

"The Significance of the Frontier in American History," Frederick Jackson Turner warned that the entrepreneurial spirit of Americans could vanish with the open prairie. Mr. Dow suspected otherwise. A tall, taciturn and bearded journalist, Charles Dow had spent his first years reporting for various newspapers in Springfield, Mass. And Providence, R. I. His early work was diligent but unexceptional. In 1879, however, when Mr. Dow was 27 years old, he was sent to cover the silver rush in Leadville, Colorado. He rode west with the president of the New York Stock Exchange and a group of financiers and journalists. In Leadville, Mr. Dow found a "gigantic lottery," where the ignorant fared as well as the educated. Astonished he wrote that "Men sprang from poverty to affluence in an hour." His letters from "the Magic City" described not only the silver ores but the rampant gambling and 82 saloons (vastly outnumbering churches). Breaking with his usual modesty, Mr. Dow observed that many mining claims bore the names of the attractive personnel of Leadville's lushly appointed brothel.

When Mr. Dow returned east, he moved to Brooklyn and struck out for Wall Street. He worked first as a mining-stock reporter, then in general financial news. After a few years he and a partner, Edward D. Jones, launched Dow Jones and Company. In 1889, they began The Wall Street Journal, with Mr. Dow as editor.

When Mr. Dow crossed the magnificent, spidery Brooklyn Bridge to Manhattan, he saw a speculative dynamism surpassing Leadville's. The streets were crowded with money men, deposited by trolley, elevated train and stage coach. There were markets for stocks, bonds commodity futures and the raw stuff itself-fresh fish and coffee beans being off-loaded by the boat full.

CHAPTER 6

Forming the Business Empire

In 1892 at the age of 29, Henry Ford constructed the first potential car for the average individual. In the first year of production his profit was $3000. Ten years later his profit was in the millions.

His idea of the assembly line production brought the car within the reach of the average individuals. His first charter shareholders were eleven individuals which included John and Horace Dodge.

Henry Ford was of Irish descent and what was unique about this was that in North Eastern Pennsylvania the Irish were brought to the area to work in the coal mines. Significantly Henry was acquainted with Thomas Edison who introduced Ford to J. P. Morgan and this acquaintance opened the door to the capital market required to move forward on the production of cars. Edison brought Ford to the attention of the New York Banking Trust led by J. Peirpoint Morgan who had partners in the coal trust representatives from North Eastern Pennsylvania who were bringing the coal trust royalties to Morgan for the purpose of investment in various businesses. Jay Gould was one of the persons sent out by the Morgan interests to seek out business opportunity for the investment capital that Morgan controlled by virtue of his relationship to the coal interests ,Gould lost favor with Morgan and the coal trust interests due to his going it alone attitude.

It should be noted that while Morgan was to invest the coal trust capital, strict criteria were laid out first and foremost that no capital was to be given to any business that might compete for the mining labor in North East Pennsylvania. It was then spelled out to Ford as to others that one place he could not set up a plant was in North Eastern Pennsylvania. Exactly how this was spelled out to Morgan is a subject of conjecture and only those that might know are gone.

Similarly John & Horace Dodge who were also capitalized by Morgan in order to provide parts for the cars and also to build the assembly line were similarly directed by the House of Morgan. Since Morgan supplied their capital he could dictate where they could locate their manufacturing plants.

Since Morgan Knew that if he violated the direction of the capital providence (i.e.) the coal trusts then the end result would be a drying up of capital for investment. A logical conclusion of the above would be that the House of Morgan by itself could not fund the numerous businesses being brought to his group except that Morgan bow to the wishes of the risk capital providers from North Eastern Pennsylvania coal royalty trusts..

John & Horace Dodge saw an opportunity to go beyond a Ford parts supplier and pressed Ford for a distribution of surplus cash as dividends. This provided part of the capital for the dodge corporation but the main investment capital came by way of the House of Morgan in the form of moneys from coal trust royalties through the banks controlled by Morgan.

Similarly in order to build the number of cars needed the House of Morgan provided the capital investment to construct the facilities for the production of tires. Here again the House of Morgan provided the capital to Frank Siberling to move this project forward in Ohio which you will recall was in the area of control of the original Connecticut corporation. Again the criteria to back Seiberling (later named the Goodyear Tire Corporation) was that he had to construct the facilities in an area that would not compete for the coal labor. While the main plant was near Akron, Ohio, Siberling was not to construct any plant of consequence in North Eastern Pennsylvania since the money would not be given to him for investment.

As you can see in these examples the power of investment capital goes far beyond the imagination of many. Studies of the flow of investment capital have always shown that the flow was from the North East to all other parts of the country even up to 1960 and beyond. Even in 1999 the studies still show capital moves from east to west.

How great a part that George Westinghouse and Thomas Edison played in the rise of the electricity and the auto industry can only be left to conjecture but it is clear that whatever part they played, there were both backed with investment capital in competition to one another by J. Peirpoint and the House of Morgan. As I mentioned all of the risk capital was received from the hard coal royalties through their trusts of which there were many but worked in concert in defiance of any antitrust laws bringing capital through their agents (partners in the House of Morgan) to bring about the creation of various businesses and Industrial giants and making them do their bidding either overtly or covertly so that the flow of investment capital to the House of Morgan could continue unimpeded.

As further described here and in previous chapters the Industrial Revolution was able to come about because of the capital and political mores, provided through the hard coal trust agents to the House of Morgan and the political power wielded by the election of 7 presidents from Ohio through the use of Mark Hanna of Ohio.

The creation of the more than 112 large corporation came about because of this abundance of capital and the shrewdness of J. P. Morgan. Significantly one might question why the flow of capital would not be in the North Eastern Pennsylvania area and create major investment and business giants in the North Eastern Pennsylvania this would be a disaster to the flow of capital since there would be no captive people to work the coal mines and continue to produce the royalties and profit to fund the House of Morgan projects.

In 1920 the height of the anthracite industry production more than 60 million in royalties went to the trusts in North East Pennsylvania. This was investment capital beyond imagination worth some 6 billion today.

The purpose of this book is to show how the United States of America was financed to grow into the industrial giant that it became during the Industrial Revolution. To show how each and every one of the industries and businesses were secretly financed by the House of Morgan using the capital derived from the coal trusts is beyond the scope of this book.

Some other examples of industry and business ventures that were financed by the coal trust royalties and profits will be examined to show that other people collaborated with the coal trusts to finance a variety of significant industries with the help of the House of Morgan. J. Peirpoint Morgan passed away in 1913 and significantly the Federal Reserve act which was in play previous was passed in 1913. It is reasonable to conclude that the interests of the coal interests and the House of Morgan would not be served by the creation of the Federal reserve because this could more tightly control the lending capability of the New York Banks and investment houses controlled by Morgan and the north east Pennsylvania coal trusts.. So it is reasonable to assume that the House of Morgan could do without the Federal Reserve system since it would cramp his style of operation and would force a revelation of the sources of investment capital that Morgan was using to establish businesses and to play one against the other as was the case of George Westinghouse and Thomas Edison. When Edison would not go along with Morgan to convert from DC to AC electric generating, Morgan removed him from the Edison General Electric Illuminating Corporation and subsequently dropped the Edison name and thus was born the General Electric Corporation a creation of the House of Morgan and money from the coal trusts. Incidentally Edison was actually born in the upper section of Ohio and was told to go to New Jersey to establish his operations for obvious reasons.

Later in 1933 the Securities act was passed by Roosevelt and this created another roadblock to the successors of Morgan and their businesses funding aspirations.

Going back to the House of Morgan, another significant indication of how cunning Morgan was in his use of the coal trust capital. Morgan using the coal trust capital funded the original French investment of 40 million in the French Panama Canal effort. Morgan could see that the French had taken on too difficult a project and convinced Theodore Roosevelt whose brother in law was Douglas Robinson a major partner of Morgan and directly related through the marriage of his daughter to John N.Conyngham II the coal trusts representative from North East Pennsylvania to bail out the French investors for the 40 million invested thus far and convinced Roosevelt to have the United States take on the project. Morgan financed the French so that the scope of the project was beyond his means of funding but wanted to get the 40 million of his coal trust investors money back. There are arguments back and forth regarding the size of Morgan's original investment with the French but he did get the 40 million back for the coal trusts. Joseph Pulitzer exposed the scheme and accused Roosevelt of taking some of the money along with Morgan and Douglas Robinson a relative of Roosevelt and a partner in the House of Morgan. This infuriated Roosevelt who threatened to sue Pulitzer but the case was never prosecuted by Roosevelt in court. The exact proof of what Pulitzer claimed was never obtained. However, the Pulitzer New Yorker would do enough damage that it caused Morgan to be more careful in his future dealings. As a reward to Roosevelt he was given the Safari to Africa. There is enough information available from other sources to indicate that Pulitzer was on the right track with his accusations concerning the 40 million invested in the Panama Canal by Morgan interests prior to the United States taking on the Panama project.

When I talk about the coal trusts it must be remembered that in other writings of a historical nature it was pointed out that the coal trusts were led by lawyers who were self taught and came from the various families that owned coal lands. In essence they were ignorant of business practices and had no business experience or acumen let alone legal expertise. The trusts were copied from old English trusts and were grand fathered when the trust laws were changed. As one person who was involved indicated to me the trusts allowed only a 5% principal reduction each year and 5% of the interest earned. On this basis the trusts could only grow and if conservatively invested could never go out of existence. As a matter of fact the growth of the trusts under this scenario is astronomical.

Thus it can be seen that with the lack of business expertise and business experience the trust lawyers (who were family members and relatives) had to rely upon others who could be trusted to invest their coal trust capital and being of a conservative nature invested through their agent in the New York Banks and Morgan's father Junius funneling the money through England into the House of Morgan and then into the various projects and thereby also the House of Morgan. Trusting Morgan and his partners in the House of Morgan to pick proper business investing for the coal industry royalties and profits. As they say the proof is in the pudding and success begets success.

Incidental to the investments in the House of Morgan within the area of North Eastern Pennsylvania the trusts owned and controlled all of the major utilities and the major banks in North East Pennsylvania through the interlocking coal trusts. In this way the coal trusts could protect the area from infringement of industry that would take away the coal mine labor. All of this being done in a way that was not obvious to the average individual. As I mentioned before this allowed control of both the individual and the politics of the area since many of the politicians who could help the coal interests were funded by the coal interests funds.

Since there are many individuals previously named in the history of the area of northeast Pennsylvania and mentioning them in writing who were significant in the area in the way of politics and industry would be redundant. Further, whether those people should get the blame or credit for their actions is beyond the scope of this book. In addition, the heirs after the decline of anthracite in post 1920 are not responsible for any detrimental factors of the past nor can they claim credit for any of the good done beyond this time. Therefore, I prefer to describe rather than name those who may have been significant in financing the United States of America. The financing was not done in a sense of altruism but was done for a self interest and while the House of Morgan took the blame for anything negative, the coal interests took the profit and avoided blame or finger pointing . While the coal trusts prospered , the United Stated of America benefited from the invest-ments. North Eastern Pennsylvania coal trusts hid in the shadows even after the decline of anthracite. This was due to the fact that the early movers in northeast Pennsylvania who worked with J. P. Morgan have long gone to their demise. The people in the trusts today basically have not the same business acumen or desire to take on the kind of responsi-bility that their predecessors did to grow North Eastern Pennsylvania let alone the United States.

In 1912 any American who would read about business knew that J. Peirpoint Morgan was a power broker in the world of money. The exact dimension of his power were sketched out by the house banking and currency committee. The House of Morgan was in effect the Central Bank of the United States. The one thing not revealed in their investiga-tion was (where was the investment capital coming from) that Morgan's risk capital was coming from anthracite coal trusts in North Eastern Pennsylvania .Some 60 million and more dollars each year were available at least from 1890 through 1930. This amount of capital created an investment house with 600 million to 60 billion per year to invest in various businesses . One significant statement made in the final Pujo investigation report was that the three life insurance companies controlled by Morgan specifically New York Life, Mutual of New York and Equitable Life needed to invest 55,000,000 .00 each year in various ventures. It was demonstrated that a few New York bankers who were really stooges of Morgan with Morgan their leader dominated banking , credit, and the stock markets in the United States through interlocking directories. Morgan men sat on the boards of the countries 112 major industries. Railroads, steel, banks, coal mines and public utilities. Morgan and his partners controlled more than 112 of the largest corporations in the United States in 1912. No one who needed a loan or a stock issue dared offend the House of Morgan. No one at that time knew essentially all of Morgan's risk equity capital came from North Eastern Pennsylvania coal trusts and banks. The House of Morgan controlled the boards of 112 United States corporations worth more than 22 billion in stock. Morgan died in 1913, probably partly as a result of the pressure he was under from the Federal Government. In 1913 the unofficial central banking authority wielded by the House of Morgan was replaced by the governments own central bank the federal reserve system. This led to the collapse of the value of the stocks controlled by Morgan and shored up by the creation of his own rating agency the Dow Jones(SEE FIG 22)group of stocks. This rating system lost its power after Morgan's death and resulted in the stock market crash of 1929 when investors lost their confidence in Morgan's son and the men left to invest the coal trust money. The federal reserve created in 1913 was not powerful enough to stabilize the situation since they had no leader of the stature of J. P. Morgan. Remember that the bankers who were appointed to the federal reserve were former stooges of J. P . Morgan and did not have the ability to think for themselves.

So great was the power of Morgan and his banking cohorts and partners from the hard coal interest in North Eastern Pennsylvania that the federal reserve system still was ruled by the district bankers since 11 of the reserve officers even today overshadowed the 7 appointed by the central government. Thus effectively establishing control of the money supply in the hands of private individuals and the bankers and this is as it should be since the government even before proved it's ineptitude with money.

In 1912 Arsene Pujo (SEE FIG 23) a congressman from Louisiana began an investigation into the dealings of J. P. Morgan to determine if J. P. Morgan had a money trust. This investigation resulted in 2,226 pages of reports concerning the investigation. The sum and substance of the reports was summarized in a final report on February 28, 1913 (SEE FIG. 1). As you know J. P. Morgan passed away in 1913 and it is believed that the strain of being investigated by the Pujo Committee resulted in J. P.'s death.

While the final report details certain committee findings unless you have other information detailed here., These are no solid conclusions about J. P. Morgan's money trust. While the committee felt strongly in the report that J. P. had a money trust they never were able to show that J. P.'s investment capital came from the coal fields in North East Pennsylvania funneled directly and through England as related in other chapters of this book. J. P. Morgan was a power broker who basically controlled all of the 112 of the largest corporation in the U. S. however the Pujo Committee was never able to show the exact way that J. P. Morgan controlled all of these corporations. J. P. Morgan hinted to the committee his power when he answered questions as to how he acquired the equitable life insurance operation. I show the exact same kind of power displayed in his acquisition of the homestead steel and iron works from Andrew Carnegie. His dismissal of Edison because he would not go to AC current and his financing of all the other examples I show in the book and his handling of the president Ted Roosevelt and others. The final Pujo report shows clearly that while he controlled enormous amounts of wealth in the 112 corporations his own investment capital paled in comparison (less than 100 million) to the amount of dollars he controlled(at least 21 billion). His money trust existed in his partners from North East Pennsylvania represented by his partners John Conyngham II, Douglas Robinson his father in law and others who funneled the money from North East Pennsylvania and brought to him the risk equity investment capital he needed to control the corporations shown in the final Pujo report which is attached for referral and study. Throughout the final Pujo report references are made to the power and control of J. P. Morgan had by the interlocking directorates all of whom were subservient to Morgan, thereby making Morgan in effect the ruler of all business transactions in the United States except for North Eastern Pennsylvania upon whom he relied for a continuous supply of investment capital. In this way he could continue to control all the business affairs of all the major corporations in the U.S. except those in North Eastern Pennsylvania who were controlled by the coal trust interests.

As stated earlier J. P. Morgan could not locate any of his industrial or other great businesses in North Eastern Pennsylvania lest he eliminate his source of continuing investment capital. His power was brought out in the final questioning of the Pujo Committee as to how he gained control of the equitable life insurance company when he told the questioner that he told Mr. Ryan of equitable that he wanted Mr. Ryan to sell his equitable stock to J. P. because J. P. said it was a good thing for J. P. to have and so Ryan sold the stock under a veiled threat from J. P.Morgan. Anyone who believed what Morgan said to the questioner is a fool.

The only people J. P. could not threaten were the representatives and trust investors from North East Pennsylvania who gave him the continuing supply of risk capital for investment which allowed J. P. to amass his great control of all the major industries, rail roads, utilities and investment houses. This allowed J. P. to be the sole arbitrator of who

47

received loans, whose stock could be issued and marketed and whose bonds could be issued and marketed. He was the make or break man of business in the United States.

The end result of the Pujo investigation was the creation of the Federal Reserve act of 1913 which came about to be implemented after J. P.'s death, and the passage of the Clayton Antitrust Act which further put safeguards against the emergence of another J. P. Morgan. From 1913 on the investment continued from the North East coal into Morgan's Bank now controlled by his son. However, his son even if he had the genius of his father J. P. could not hold together the businesses with the tight grip and shrewd deals that his father had accomplished. It is very likely that because of these events Federal Reserve Act and Clayton Antitrust act and the death of J. P. Morgan this eventually led to the stock market crash in 1929 since the shrewdness of J. P. and his control of stock prices through Dow also was lost after 1913. This is likened to a ship sailing without a captain, Eventually disaster strikes and the ship will go down. A careful reading of the final Pujo report will confirm the above.

The elder Morgan through his connections with Philadelphia interests formed an association with who he thought could guide the Connecticut Yankees with their new found land wealth. He came upon the idea of using acquaintances from Philadelphia who came up to North Eastern Pennsylvania and took a lead role in guiding the Connecticut farmers as to how to protect and enhance their new found wealth in the form of coal royalties. This resulted in the Conyngham ,Wells ,and Hollenback families becoming the leading interests in North Eastern Pennsylvania to guide the investment of capital growing in the trust royalties. It was the consortium of people along with the Cooperation of others that continued from the elder Morgan Junius and magnified itself with his son J. P. Morgan's brilliance in arranging the financial deals that led to the Industrial Revolution (which was helped by way of a 40% import tariff arranged by his political connections through Mark Hanna and others) where in he melded together such people as (Mark Hanna from Ohio) who arranged at the behest of the coal trusts and Morgan to elect 7 presidents of the United States from Ohio who would assist them in carrying out their investments with little interference from the central government until the death of J. P. Morgan and the advent of the 1930's when anthracite coal was dead for all practical purposes. This changed the emphasis of investment of coal royalties which now became speculative deals and without the leadership and business acumen of a J. P. Morgan resulted in safer investments through the consortium of banks they controlled and the utilities and other safer investments.

John N. Conyngham II and Hayfield House (SEE FIG 21)

Hayfield House outside of Wilkes-Barre, Pa. Now serves as the administrative offices of Penn State University Wilkes-Barre Campus. The 55 room mansion was built by John N. Conyngham II during the depression for approximately one million dollars.

John N. Conyngham II and Douglas Robinson were both partners of J. P. Morgan. Hayfield House contained 55 rooms with 12 fireplaces and bathroom fixtures made of gold.

The stone dwelling with Vermont slate roof, Tibetan room, a federalist room, a floating staircase and a dressing room modeled after Marie Antionette's boudoir.

The three story mansion was the summer home of Bertha Robinson (Douglas Robinson's daughter) wife of John N. Conyngham II. It was completed in 1933 however John N. passed away in 1930. Bertha his wife lived to nearly 100 and used the estate for a summer home until 1964.

In the Wall Street Journal in 1985 there was a study to determine who the land owners of the original 13 colonies were today in 1999 It was determined that Tennessee should be studied and the results applied to all the colonies. They found that 60% of the ground was owned by the original people granted land. If you carry that logic further as they did, they came to the conclusion that it Tennessee was still owned by the same people they made the conclusion, erroneous or not, that the sixty percent or more of the ground in the original thirteen colonies is today still owned by the descendants of the same people. This seems to be logical and maybe it can be questioned, but it seems to be logical. Furthermore, they came to the basic and logical conclusion that he who controls the ground upon which people live also controls the destiny of those people who live on their ground, particularly the economic destiny of those people who live on that ground and that's important to keep in mind when we're going through further chapters in this book and it will further, I think, explain the mentality of the people who today reside in what is known as North Eastern Pennsylvania and which was the only place in the United States in which there was anthracite hard coal. Now another thing that can be tied in with the Wall Street Journal study that was reported could be another study made and reported in our local North East Pennsylvania newspaper and this can be utilized in explaining something that is true today as it was I believe it also true at the time that the first settlers from Connecticut obtained the ground in North Eastern Pennsylvania and the rights and ownership to the ground in North Eastern Pennsylvania and to the coal that lay beneath that ground .That study reported to say the way that people obtain positions of employment and I dare say favored positions too for example people in business just don't happenstance get an opportunity. I think when I relate the study you will see that more than likely the same thing goes on in business but this was a study about how people get jobs in our current time period of nineteen nineties. Interestingly enough it was discovered that statistically eighty-five percent of the people who get jobs get them because they were referred, and some might say that they got it through influence, but well referred does not necessarily mean influence and the explanation of this study was that the reason that eighty-five percent get the jobs by referral is that you've got to understand that if a person comes in the door as reportedly fifteen percent do and without any reference fill out on an application for a position and go in and see the personnel director or the owner and say I'd like to have a job in this organization. Now it doesn't seem likely that, especially for a high position, that they would just take that person as he walked through the door on face value even if his credentials are good and hire him for that position .There are two reasons why, number one if the person is referred to the personnel director or to the owner or to a subordinate and that person works out good, then that person can take credit not the person giving the reference but the person doing the hiring for that person doing good and so he can bask in that pride. However if that person fails in that position then there's a scapegoat the person who referred him. So I believe that is the rational explanation of why eighty-five percent of people who get positions get them by reference from the lowest laborer to the highest executive. So that being the case doesn't it seem to be foolish to be in the fifteen percent category however if we look at that study and look back into the early eighteen hundreds why would the people who owned the ground and who owned the coal underneath and who have royalties coming from the coal underneath why would they give an opportunity to someone they didn't know, it doesn't even seem logical so who did they know? They knew other high Episcopalians, high Presbyterians, or low Presbyterians or low Episcopalians but they knew them. They didn't particularly look on the Welsh as entrepreneurs but looked at them as workers. So if an opportunity presented itself it generally was not offered to the Welsh person but there were exceptional cases but in general what they would look for is some of their own kind Episcopalians or Presbyterians who appeared to have the business ability and if they had the proper expertise to carry forward the project ,.using the Welsh workers and their ingenuity their engineering ability and work ability, using those people to create the colliery then to create the houses that the people live in and create the churches bring in the church people so that they could keep them in line. Then bringing in the stores so they could feed them and bringing in transportation of one kind or another. Horse drawn trolleys originally and from then on into the trolleys and then to electric and gas buses. So those two studies I think explain what happened in the early eighteen hundreds through these people of brilliance who were directing if not they themselves the Connecticut Yankees had the ingenuity. They knew enough to go and find somebody who had the business acumen in Philadelphia and bring them up here and take them in as partners. Still maintaining control of the ground and maybe giving them some of the ground as a bonus to keep them in with them. Now in some cases they were outsmarted (I'm talking about the Connecticut Yankees) by the others who they brought in and I'll later point out some of those examples where the people they brought in actually over shadowed them but you have to understand if a person of the oak tree charter was a businessman then he had the acumen to put together the business but if he was a farmer then he didn't have the acumen to put together the business so some were businessmen some were farmers some were ordinary people in this corporation and so in order to carry forward this economic prosperity that they hit upon and to devise ways of keeping soft coal for example and the oil and the gas under wraps until such time as they can be utilized took tremendous intelligence and keenness and cunningness and it's difficult to say from the information that is available who was the businessman who was the entrepreneur who was the farmer, but we can speculate about that and we can from certain information that we have available we can tie it together and we'll try to detail that out in succeeding chapters. There are other things we can include from the era of eighteen hundred to eighteen forty where the actual impetus to move the anthracite coal out of North Eastern Pennsylvania and into the economy of the United States actually began and if you take that forty years just as example and compare it to the last forty years from 1950 until 1995 there is no comparison in our area here as far as economic prosperity because the economic prosperity that came about from eighteen hundred to eighteen forty in our area was tremendous compared to our forty years here going back from 1995 and so it's an interesting comparison. I wonder if we even compared any other area of the United States forty years back whether the same acceleration of economic growth was apparent anywhere else. Certainly it was not apparent anywhere else in the United States at that time even if we in another chapter when we compare the period of growth from 1840-1870. That's another thirty years you're going to see that there is another tremendous period of economic growth in North Eastern Pennsylvania in the way of anthracite production and a further great period of growth in the United States and we were able to show that it was a direct result of the moneys that were to flow from the anthracite and in other chapters we showed some other things that related to the usage of the flow of money from the anthracite but going back to the 1800-1840 period. Now you have to remember that the Wyoming Valley was known early as the Westmoreland County of Connecticut, Before the Pennamite wars were fought and finally settled. You have to remember then that as the coal was found and developed from 1800-1840 and beyond you have to remember that we can not trace exactly how the money was distributed and what trusts it went into early and even as in today we only know smatterings of what trusts exists and what they control and to what extent they are since we don't have access to the trusts we have memorandum that a trust may exist in the court but we can not really know what it is. For example, one of the people that was involved in one of the trusts told me that the trusts, which were basically all set up the same way, by designation were detailed to distribute only five percent of the income and five percent of the principal if that were so it would be a situation that would be an ongoing trust it would continue to grow and never diminish even if anthracite went out of existence as an example look at the Kirby trust which had nothing to do with anthracite and I will go into them in detail later and show how the Kirby trust came about from the Kirby family and F. W. Woolworth stores and how the Kirby stores came about. I'll briefly touch on that and how it related to the economics of the anthracite but as an example one trust that the Kirby family set up for charitable purposes in 1930, when it was set up, had only approximately 5-8 million in it and today even after giving away millions and millions and today they give away eight to ten million a year has in excess of one hundred and sixty-five million in the trust. Going back to the period before I leave it to 1800-1840 I am going to detail out a number of names and what we think their early involvement was in the Connecticut land grants the oak tree charter and maybe so called coal baron syndrome so the period from 1800-1840 was a very significant period in the rise and fall of anthracite coal and also in the rise and fall of canals and inland waterways as a method of cheap and convenient transportation for around 1838 the demand for anthracite coal was so great that the canals were over-whelmed and this gave rise to the influx of rail into North Eastern Pennsylvania to bring the black gold to market now another thing we ought to look at in the period from 1800-1840 is who were the shakers and the movers and the bigger cities that existed at that time which was primarily New York City and Philadelphia and we will mention what our thoughts are on those matters but from what we can determine to this point there were no real shakers and movers in that period of time and any moneys that came into New York or Philadelphia came from three sources one was from England the other from Europe and the other was from North Eastern Pennsylvania coal trusts and profits, those were the only areas where money could come from there was excess money for investment from England and there was excess money for investment from Europe and particularly France but by and large from what we can determine the greatest amount of capital that was available for risk capital was from North Eastern Pennsylvania from the production of anthracite.

CHAPTER 7

The Rise and Fall of King Coal

In the year 1900-1920 the usage of oil in the car and further in the air-plane and further in the usage of oil in power generation and during the war usage of oil in tanks and a myriad of uses that began to come about because of the refining processes continued to expand the usage of oil and the demand for oil. However the tremendous demand for coal was still apparent and it will show in the statistics available during that period that the production of oil rose with the production of coal and these conflicting capacities competed with one another and in 1920 the epitome of the anthracite industry more than 120 million tons of anthracite coal were produced in Luzerne county alone. The entire anthracite field produced in excess of 120 million. All of this coal was in demand for a myriad of uses because the advent of producing gas from coal was still in play and the pipelines for low BTU gas were already in place in certain areas. Not until later would the actual expansion of the transcontinental gas lines take place from Texas and Oklahoma but in the period between 1900-1920 the massive amount of revenue from the coal was placed in the trusts through the vehicle of trust deeds which defined the coal vein from which coal was extracted required a royalty of approximately .50 a ton and even to this day the royalty was paid whenever coal was strip mined. In this period of time also some giants of industry were beginning to prosper and emerge primarily financed by the business interests of the coal people and their ingenuity and their ability to take advantage of the growing times was unique in the history of the United States. As an example after the World War I Mr. Carpenter was sent down by the coal trusts with certain monies to Dupont corporation who were in trouble financially and through agreements he essentially controlled the Dupont Corporation. He later married a Dupont person and was well known in the Wyoming Valley area for his contribution in the Dupont area and his allegiance to the moneyed interests who sent him down to the Dupont Corporation to take control essentially of the Dupont Corporation. At this time General Motors corporation was expanding and with the knowledge that Mr. Carpenter had invested in General Motors through the Dupont Corporation. It wasn't until approximately 1947 when new and stronger anti—trust laws came into being that the government went after the Dupont Corporation to divest of what they considered a Dupont monopoly .This resulted in a divestiture of the general motors by Dupont corporation however the stock ended up in the hands of the original owners through the hidden trusts. Another person who I can mention from the Wyoming Valley coal collieries was a family known by the name of the Dorrance . Col. John Dorrance who was the actual operator of at least two collieries and amassed a fortune in the amount of approximately 120 million dollars. He subsequently died and left that money to his son John Dorrance II. John Dorrance II in the meantime also inherited a fledgling condensed soup company in Camden New Jersey (the Campbell soup company) that his father had started .The son invested in other ventures which lost approximately 40 million dollars and then he abandoned those efforts and concentrated on the condensed soup known as the Campbell soup company with plants in Camden, New Jersey. With the concentration on the condensed soup John Dorrance moved to be closer to the operation from the Wyoming Valley down to the Philadelphia area and further made his home from that point on in the Philadelphia area never letting it be known that his original money stake came from coal profits and that his roots were in the Wyoming valley in Northeastern Pennsylvania . He prospered and rose to be a billionaire written up in Fortune magazine. He was married and his wife and he had four children, two girls and two boys, who I will relate later as to what happened to those people. Another person who came to prominence from the anthracite coal and was a beneficiary of the funds that were derived from anthracite coal, this was a person by the name of Kirby who came to the Wyoming Valley more or less penniless and who through some influence (which I can't determine at this time) was befriended by the coal trust interests into starting what was known as the Kirby five and dime stores and he masterfully worked those stores into a great expansion and financial success backed financially by the coal interests and he subsequently merged with the assistance of the House of Morgan with the Wool Worth Corporation. He actually amassed a fortune, he further was such a brilliant businessman and with the backing of these people formed the Alleghany Corporation in which they invested in various other ventures outside of the Wool Worth Corporation and to this day his family and his descendants took control of the wealth they had and intelligently I might say invested their money into financial planning and ended up as one of the major mergers. They became one of the major owners of American Express. Incidentally, this Kirby family was a very charitable family they never really mined any coal but had a great love for the Wyoming Valley and a relationship with the people who provided them with their early financial benefit which enabled them to move so brilliantly forward in the business world and are known for many charitable ventures and in fact one of the Kirby's set up a trust in the 1930's with the amount of 8 million dollars and it grew from the 8 million into today about 160 million dollars .They give away approximately 8 million dollars a year to various charities. Another venture of the anthracite people in which they invested was the Union Pacific railroad and to this day they have an interest in the union pacific. Due to the nature of the trusts it's very difficult to establish the actual worth of the various coal trusts that were established. Another person that had done rather well in the coal industry was a person by the name of Haddock .They were known as the Haddock collieries in the Wyoming Valley .He and his wife had two daughters and they were the beneficiaries of his estate and it's been reported (I learned that the through one of the coal trust people who were privy to this information) that the girls in that period of time approximately 1900 inherited a sum of tax exempt bonds which were paying approximately one percent interest at the time .Two lawyers had to spend two days every six months clipping the coupons and cashing them in which reportedly gave them an income in 1900 of six thousand dollars per day. Now it's been reported that these two sisters one of them moved down to North Carolina and was involved in a farm and loved sheep and had little cabins made for each one of the sheep and had gold plates put on with their names and servants taking care of the sheep. The other daughter it's been reported was a philanthropist and gave the money to restore Martha Washington's home on Long Island. It's difficult to really trace down all of the people who might have been involved in businesses other than the coal field and investments that were made but we know that the money was firstly invested through J. P. Morgan to control the major corporations in the United States of America. However it's certainly a sure thing that the utilities the water, gas lines, water company, electric company in the North Eastern part of Pennsylvania were owned and controlled principally by coal and land owners intermingled with the coal trusts. Furthermore all of the banks (the major banks in the area) were set up and controlled by the coal interests. So it was rather difficult if you were involved in the coal industry it would be very difficult to obtain financing for other ventures unless they were assured (the banks) that there was no threat of more or less stealing of the company employees of the various coal collieries because it was basically a situation where if they were to give you the money they were biting off their nose to spite their face. So all of the ventures of great importance and investments were made through intermediaries whom they trusted and one of those was Jay Gould. Jay Gould was written up in history as an entrepreneur, but he really had nothing. He was a scout for the coal interests and for J. P. Morgan and the person who was to find out various businesses to invest in .He was given authority to do certain investments and was backed by the money interests to fund various ventures that he suggested they get involved with. Another person as mentioned before who remained in the area was Asa Packer. Asa Packer was the person who brought in the Lehigh valley rail roads and was responsible for most of the rail road tracks coming into the area to take the coal out. Any other rail roads that came into the area was by virtue of a franchise from coal interests. So the time from 1900 to 1920 was the last hurrah of the coal industry and during that period of time there were a lot of financial accomplishments by the moneyed and coal industry's trusts.. And as you compare the coal interest people and the way they invested their money compared to the owner and founder of the New York Central Rail Road which was owned by Commodore Vanderbilt and his family you'd find two contrasting methods of operation and also a situation in New York Central where the family is not protected by trusts and as a matter of fact the failure of the New York Central rail road and the bankruptcy of it left the heirs with nothing. One example of how foolish some of the heirs could be, one heir went down to North Carolina and with his millions of dollars of inheritance proceeded without any figuring out how the additional moneys were to come his way built a tremendous mansion and before he even got the mansion finished he had to borrow additional moneys to finish it and by that time he found out he had no money to run it and he ended up losing the mansion that he bought and today it stands as a monument to the folly of one of the Vanderbilts.

And it's a show place now for tourists. The Vanderbuilt fortune was parceled out to the inheritors and when the New York Central Rail Road went bankrupt that was all that was left for the inheritors was what came out of the bankruptcy and that was very little. And contrast that with the coal interests even into today there is still money going into the trusts and the trusts are building up in value and the trusts are limited in the distribution as I mentioned earlier in one of the other trusts so that the trusts grow constantly instead of being depleted. Now even the Rockefeller trusts were not set up properly. For example recently half of the Rockefeller center was sold to Japanese interests for one billion dollars and the reasoning behind that is that the inheritors who have no resemblance many of them to a Rockefeller name indicated that they were running out of money to give away and so that was their reason for selling (which was a foolish reason). Contrast that with the coal interest, the inheritors are not allowed to tell the lawyers who handle the coal trust what assets to sell and what assets to keep. And continuing to concentrate some of the effort into the 1900-1920 period this was a period of great change with regard to North Eastern Pennsylvania because the reliance on coal was soon to diminish and the inheritors (actually the inheritors of the second and third generations) of the trusts realized this also and the latter part of the 1920's began to try to find ways of disposing or selling off the coal interests . Now the oil interest had already been working into the Texas fields and so the coal interests began to expand the Western Pennsylvania fields and Ohio fields by their man Rockefeller to get the gas and oil out of the ground and to market. So their vision was in the right direction and they made their moves in the direction of other assets as I mentioned before like the Dupont venture, the Union Pacific, Worthington Industries, the AT&T, the Pennsylvania Power and Light, Pennsylvania Enterprises, and telephone companies were those kind of things that their moneys that had been built in the trust could be protected against inflation and loss. There were investments made from the coal interests during this period in stocks. A great many of their investments were into tax exempt bonds which were issued by the municipal governments and even though they gave very little interest there was no tax in the United States to be lost to the government .The income tax came into play in 1930 and so up until the time that the income tax came into play there was no dissipation of the moneys that continued to pour in from the various collieries that were mining the coal, which as I mentioned before .50 a ton went to various trusts from every vein of coal that was mined. Interestingly enough even through this period of time there were additional rail systems which came into play such as the Delaware-Lackawanna, Wyoming, the Jersey Central, New York Central as I mentioned before, Pennsylvania rail road, it's difficult to understand what amount of ownership in these rail roads came back into the trusts. But for the right to move into the area and get the ground upon which they could lay their tracks. They would have had to give them stock or cash and I would assume that they were given stock rather than cash in these railroads. In this period of time from 1900-1920 the unions in the coalfields began to come into play. However the earliest attempted unionization was in Schuylkill county by the Irishman Black jack Kehoe who for his efforts of unionizing the workers known as the Molly Macguires, he was hung on a trumped up charge by the judge in order to protect the coal interests from unionization. They had to get rid of the leader of the Molly Macguires and so they trumped up the charge on Black Jack Kehoe to keep them down. However in the 1900-1920 period Mitchell came into play and then later John L. Lewis to organize the United Mine Workers and at first it was a difficult thing to organize them because their was great animosity towards unionization of the coal workers, both by the inheritors and the colliery owners. There has to be a distinction made here between the colliery operators and the inheritors. In some cases the colliery operators were the inheritors and in other cases the colliery operators were rendered that favoritism by the inheritors only the inheritors rendered that favoritism those upon whom. It's difficult to prove which was which because of the intermarriage that took place much similar, to what took place in England. In the period from 1900-1920 I mentioned the oil was pumped out of Texas and already Rockefeller by the fact that he was given money from the coal trust interests through Morgan to purchase oil companies began to put up refineries and the motorized vehicles that utilized gas and oil came into being especially with World War I and so there was an explosion of activity utilizing oil and gas after World War I and so this was another impetus to inheritors and the coal interest people to move in the direction of oil and gas, utilities and other ventures. So as I mentioned earlier when the Dupont interest was acquired they also acquired the General Motors interest and of course gave the coal interests another thing to fall back on when the hard coal lost its economic luster.

CHAPTER 8

The Period of Economic Decline

War From 1920 to 1945 there was a continuous decline in production of anthracite until World II there was a spurt of activity, however it was never to reach again what the production was in 1920. Remember that out of every ton of coal produced of record fifty cents went to the coal trusts. In my correlation between the gross national product, the budget, and expenditures of the United States the amount of money that I believe may have been in the coal interest trusts was found to give an indication of what the power was of the coal trust interests.

Now in this period of time that I mentioned, there was also an explosion of car production by Henry Ford who through his friendship with Edison was financed by J.P. Morgan. Ford began to produce cars, hopefully, that each individual family could afford to buy. That was his hope. We mentioned before that the funds to back Henry Ford came from J. P. Morgan's coal trust money. There were other car companies that came into being around the same period of time that Henry Fords company did and I believe the moneyed interests through the House of Morgan invested in those other car company ventures.

In this same period of time in, the early twenties, there was a formation by the moneyed interests from coal and the eastern financial interests who got together with the coal trust interests to discuss the possible loss of value of their financial interest and control in the banking industry. Fearing that the central government or the politicians might destroy the value of the paper dollar (which was still backed at that time by some gold) they decided that they must act and so in order to protect their paper dollar interests they got together politically and through their political connections formed the federal reserve in 1913. The formation of the federal reserve was primarily accomplished to protect the integrity of the American dollar. There was a feeling at the time that politicians, if they were left to their own resources, could destroy the country, the economy, and the value of money (paper dollars) by foolishly deflating the currency. So the idea of setting up the federal reserve, which was really a private operation with some government interest, but to this day the government does not control the federal reserve, it's visa versa, the federal reserve controls the government. I am a firm believer that this is the way it should be. The idea of politicians controlling how much money is run through the presses at any one time is foolishness and the politicians would destroy the country if that were continued.

In the early thirties the handwriting was already on the wall with regard to the decline of the anthracite coal industry. We see the money interests from coal cooperating with the New York and Philadelphia bankers particularly New York and taking in partners in the banking industry in New York City. One that comes to mind that is well known is J. P. Morgan's son who was a partner of local coal interest people and from all that can be gathered it appears that J. P. Morgan was funded by the coal interests and not visa versa however as he became more astute and broke away from the coal interests and more or less outsmarted them then he didn't need to rely on them any further. During this time too the Kirby interests were being funded by the coal trust interests and expanded the Kirby stores and then merged with Frank Wool Worth to form the Woolworth Corporation. How much stock the coal trust interests received for their investment in Kirby is not known but I would guess that there's a substantial interest there into the Wool Worth Corporation .For their financial investments in Kirby they were able to garner other interests with Kirby into the Allegheny Corporation and others. These were all public corporations but at that time it would be difficult to show the exact interests of the coal trusts in the other Kirby ventures. However it is very difficult to prove the exact interest because the coal trusts were individuals as well as cooperatives and they had to be careful that they were not attacked by the government with regard to the anti-trust laws that were now being implemented. So the coal trusts operated together, but yet they also operated alone and in most cases they operated alone and only when their interests were threatened, I will give you some examples of that, when they vote together. During the period from 1920 to 1930 the coal interest trusts were operating with the son of Morgan after his fathers death in 1913 and they concentrated on investments in areas that had little or nothing to do with coal. They now recognized that the future profits were in steel, and oil, and gas, and in utilities.

In the later part of 1920 to 1930 the great depression came about. There was a stock market crash and subsequent depression, however in the North Eastern part of Pennsylvania that depression did not hit home because there was still quite a lot of coal production comparatively and so there were jobs available. There was no apple selling on the corners of the streets of North Eastern Pennsylvania. Aside from the coal industry there were other industries supported by these coal trust interests that weathered the stock market crash because their money was not as I mentioned before primarily invested in stocks, it was invested in other business such as utilities etc. They could weather that storm of depression because they did not need to cash in their stock whatever stock they owned and in many cases they were de facto owners of the enterprises in which they invested.

In the period from 1930 to 1945 coal production continued to decline, however there was still in every ton of coal there was a fifty cents royalty going to the coal trusts so there was a constant flow of cash into the coal trusts and there was a need to invest that money. During World War II there was another spurt of coal production with additional funds going into the coal trusts. In the mean time the coal trusts were majority owners of the banking facilities in North Eastern Pennsylvania and while they could not be shown to be interlocking trusts they controlled the economy of North Eastern Pennsylvania and thereby controlled the chamber of commerce and controlled those industries who they would want to bring into the area of northeast Pennsylvania. Now between 1930 and 1940 there was some interest by the local chambers of commerce in looking at the possibility of what the future might hold. And so there was a loosening up on the tight control of keeping other competing industries out that would require labor, cheap labor, or abundant labor whichever you might describe it as. However with the unionism of the coal mines the miners began to get more benefits and better wages and so the miners had a decent living if they were working in the mines. While in the later part of thirty up near forty as you know World War II began and with the Roosevelt administration there was an impetus to provide the allies in Northern France with the wares of war and so even though oil and gas were pushing to get a start there was a great need for coal still and so production continued in that period of time and into the World War II years to supply the military machine. As a matter of fact the low BTU gas did not go out of existence until some later years till the interstate gas pipelines came into existence. Low BTU gas was formed by converters that had a bed of burning anthracite coal and you could only use anthracite coal, steam was sprayed through the coal bed and this steam resulted in the manufacture of a low BTU gas. This gas was compressed in to big tanks and the weights on the tank pumped the gas, this forced the gas through large pipes for home or cooking gas, and initially lighting gas and later it began to replace the coal stokers and hand fired coal furnaces with the advent of gas fired furnaces. Now you have to remember that the coal stokers, and coal fired furnaces were in existence throughout the United States. During this period of time that we've gone over one state after another came into the union and they all needed the same thing. They needed items to move forward. They needed rails, they needed coal, they needed homes and they needed money and the money continued to flow from the east and the primary source of the abundant risk capital was the money from the coal trusts funneled through Morgan's son. So the coal trusts continued from 1930-1945 to rely on the people within the coal producing area of North Eastern Pennsylvania namely Luzerne, Lackawanna, North Umberland, Schullkill, Carbon and Wayne counties. Those areas needed sources of employment for the people within and the only source of employment (since other industry was being kept out) until World War II was the coalmine. There was an economic necessity of requiring the labor of the people within the coalmines, who had been imported earlier during the late migration. It was necessary to keep those people employed and in order to keep them employed they had to continue to try to continue the uses of anthracite. However the hand writing was on the wall for the demise of the coal industry but the usage of coal for low BTU and the usage of coal during the war effort of 1939-1945 caused a continuation of the production of anthracite coal, while production went down, coal was still needed and it was still a viable item of industry and a vital employer in North Eastern Pennsylvania.

CHAPTER 9

Hard Times in Northeastern Pennsylvania

Hard Times for the North Eastern Pennsylvania people but not the Coal Trusts

Once the war had ended the soldiers came back to North Eastern Pennsylvania and many of them looked for jobs in the coalmines, but the jobs were not there. The soldiers came back and the mines were going down, the moneyed interests and the inheritors had invested their money out of the area. The banks still owned by the trusts were reluctant to fund new ventures. There was not a unified effort to change the North Eastern Pennsylvania economy from coal to a diversified economy. After World War II there began an effort somewhat backed by the coal interest, but because of their diehard nature and since there was still some coal production there was not a full effort mounted by the moneyed interests to realize that there had to be something done to

68

maintain jobs in the area. And so after the world war 2, many of the young men in the area went to New Jersey and to Detroit and to Ohio to seek employment because there were no jobs in northeast Pennsylvania. Some men also went to New York (upper New York State) to seek work in the factories which had been built with coal trust money during the era of J.P. Morgan. The factories as earlier mentioned were deliberately shut out of our area because the labor was designated for anthracite production and the control of the moneys that would be required to invest in any new industry was always shut out by the board of directors of the banks with chamber of commerce working hand in hand with the coal trusts continued to keep the status quo.

Now from 1945 to 1960 there was a change. Slowly there was somewhat of an effort mounted to create an industrial park up in the Scranton area and down in the Wilkes-Barre area and down in the Schuylkill County area and there was an effort mounted with the funding by moneyed interests and by local people to try to solicit certain industry to come into the area. The prime beneficiary of that solicitation were low paying, low skilled jobs, non-creative type of industries initially. The garment industry was then solicited to move in from New York city with their low-paying jobs however the I.L.G.W.U. had organized in the 1930's to 1945 and they moved into our area (as the factories moved in) to organize the workers who were primarily women. Women sew the materials in the factories. So the factories came here primarily with the same set up as they had in the loft type arrangements in Philadelphia and New York city, low quality buildings, low quality facilities operating on a shoe string because the Italian and the Jewish element controlled the production of those goods from the New York area and so there had to be only a certain amount of money that could be spent on putting the goods together and while it was higher in New York because the New York cost of living was higher when they moved the production to North Eastern Pennsylvania they naturally paid less to get the goods done and that was the incentive to move to this area because there was a cheap and abundant supply of labor, poorly organized, union and non-union.

1952 to 1960 there was a greater push for industry to come into the area, however it was poorly organized due to the fact that the coal mines had left scars and pits and unstable areas within the valley. These were very poor conditions for the enticement of industry into the area. In addition to that the area had very few parcels of level ground that were not mine spoiled so there was a push on by the politicians in the state to fill in the mine voids and to level off some of the colliery banks and beautify them and this went on up until the time of 1960. During this period of time the money investments that had been made by the inheritor trusts was being multiplied dramatically because the industries outside the area of North Eastern Pennsylvania were mushrooming in growth except for a slight lull in 1958. . Further more there was a great need for additional roadways throughout the country and the interstate highway system act was passed during the Eisenhower administration and this gave rise to dramatic improvement in the economy and the mushrooming of work. However in the valley in the North Eastern part of Pennsylvania the coal producing areas there was still basically poor work conditions and availability. During all of this time in 1945 to 1960 there was tremendous growth in the area of television and the area of car production and in the area of other manufacturing, and in the area of home building industry. None of this took place in North Eastern Pennsylvania and the coal producing areas.

CHAPTER 10

What Does the Future Hold for Northeastern Pennsylvania

In 1960 President Kennedy was elected to office. The first Catholic president of the United States. He talked of a vision for the country however we have a short lived situation as he was assassinated in 1963. Now in 1960 for all practical purposes coal production was nil and the prime industry in the Wyoming valley was the garment industry, various retail enterprises etc. There was still a lack of coordinated effort in bringing in new industry into the area. The moneyed coal interests who controlled the banks were not willing to risk great amounts of capital on their own area and further more there was interest in controlling who came into the area. There was not an interest here because of the fact that the people here as you know from the previous chapters owned all of the above ground and they lived here and they were not interested in pushing forward the idea of a great influx of other people particularly unskilled people. Other ventures did not appear outside of the real estate within the northeastern part of Pennsylvania. There did not appear to be any interest by the inheritors in accumulating mass items of real estate they didn't see this as an area of production of great wealth and so they stayed away from that kind of thing and concentrated on those items which are needed for the sustenance of life which are the utilities. Because of the nature of the secrecy involved in these trusts and because of the fact that whatever intermingling of the coordination between these trusts was taking place there was naturally secrecy and so the ability to delve into the minds of these people and to find out exactly what they were doing at any particular time is not something that can be done very easily. During the 1960 to 1970 time frame there was still some effort put forth to try and change the economy of the area from stagnating and declining coal industry to a diversified type of industry, however, this was not to be carried forward expeditiously. To get an industry to come into an area that had a declining population and a declining economy base was difficult at best. There were certain kinds of industries now that the garment industries were here which paid low wages and which employed a tremendous number of people that had lost their jobs through the coal mine or had substitute jobs, the fact of loss of coal production was not an incentive to put those people out of businesses there were competing interests trying to regulate who should come in and who shouldn't come into the area in the way of industry. There was some commercial effort put forth but not until 1972 when the great Agnes flood hit was there a rebirth of economic activity as far as the commercial growth. The malls that came into the area, indoor malls both in Wilkes-Barre and in Scranton and then later in the Frackville, Pottsville area that were similar to the kinds that were being put up some years previous in other parts of the country. So there was that kind of commercial activity going on however, the financing for these ventures primarily came from other areas or was not native kind of financing because the controlling interest of the banks up until the advent of interstate banking was still the moneyed interests from the coal inheritors and their vision to say the least was myopic.

In the early nineteen seventies redevelopment authorities began to change the face of the northeastern coal producing areas in a way that had not happened for 150 years. New enterprises sprang up; new commercial ventures came about. New roads, new water systems, new sewer systems and this was all for the better. For all practical purposes coal production was nil and in my graphical approach you will see that the actual influence of coal production and the money that came from coal was practically non-existent. However, the influence of the moneyed interest and the trusts were still apparent within the coal producing areas. Not until the advent of interstate banking and the merger of banks from out of the area was there any loosening up of capital and even to the present time 1998 the banks such as Mellon bank, PNC, Meridian First Union all were moved into the area and took over the control of the moneyed interests banks. Incidentally, it's apparent in many cases that the coal trusts just exchanged stock into the larger banks, however, the fact of the matter is that they lost control of the local area by losing the banking control. So it might be said that the advent of interstate banking might have brought a greater input by developers, creativity and commercial activity but that's not the case and that's not due to the money interest or the major banks. They as much as the local people in the coal producing areas never realized that they were serfs so the money banks that moved into the area never realized that either and never gave a thought to whether or not they should be responsible for the areas growth and we don't believe that they should be in essence, however, I believe that the advent of interstate banking leveled the playing field somewhat and gave an opportunity for those who might have a creative idea a chance to fund it. One negative thing came into being that put a damper on this situation and closed the door to economic opportunity and that was the banking law of 1989 where the banking system laws were tightened up because of the savings and loan scandal and this reflected not only in our area in Northeastern Pennsylvania, but all across the country. The banking system which traditionally loaned money and as I mentioned earlier that's how all the creativity and expansion took place in the United States, now reversed itself. Now the major banks invested in treasury securities of the United States government in order to protect their asset and capital base of which there are certain significant tight requirements on those under the 1989 banking law (which I incidentally think is a poor law and has poor consequences). Since 1989 the investment of banks in commercial enterprises has gone down significantly and now the major lenders of capital to commercial and industrial enterprises are not banks but sources such as IT&T, Capital, USL Capital subsidiary of Ford, AT&T capital, Greyhound Capital Financing, Hill Financial, GE Capital those kinds of enterprises are providing the major amount of credit to enterprises across the United States and in order for the North Eastern part of Pennsylvania to survive and prosper and come into the twentieth century it will require those people, the Chambers of Commerce, who to some extent are still controlled by the moneyed interests and trust, but who have to shed those shackles and have to realize that the capital for the creative enterprises that are required is not going to come from the banks even though the banks in North Eastern Pennsylvania are now owned by other major banks as I mentioned before such as Mellon and PNC, Meridian and others now we have seen the influx of Nat West and others are beginning to realize that there are opportunities here, but there are certain others inhibitions in the banking system that prevent someone like Citibank for example to come into our area or some of the other major banks. There are other inhibiting factors to growth in our area involving the mentality of the people. Bishop O'Connor was the bishop of Scranton in the Scranton Diocese for only seven months in our area. He is now Cardinal O'Connor and went back to New York and served as the Cardinal of the Diocese of New York. Now serving in St. Patrick's Cathedral on Fifth Avenue. While he was here within the seven months at least three times in public he mentioned that the area people in the Scranton Diocese lack self-esteem. Now if you contrast the people of Scranton Diocese in character and morality, stability and industry with the people of New York city you would find they would beat the people of New York city on all counts because New York city can be called the sewer of the world in that the crime rate, the poverty rate, the lack of facilities the crampedness all contribute to a decadence of life yet the creativity is a hundred fold greater in New York city than it is in our area. I attribute this to the fact that the people here do as he said lack self-esteem and the reason they lack self-esteem, which was not mentioned by Cardinal O'Connor or some other people who had mentioned the same thing. The reason they lack self-esteem goes back to exactly what I pointed out in earlier chapters of how our area was set up. It was set up as a serfdom. Just as the kings of England had their castles, the wealthy people of England had their castles and around their castles they had the serfs working for them and the collieries were set up that way and it stays in the minds of the peoples in our area. I'm going to go through and I'm going to give examples of people who moved out of our area and lost that inhibition of lack of self-esteem and created or gathered together and pushed ahead with their creativity and self-esteem such as Mr. William McGowan who fought against all odds against AT&T and was the prime person responsible for the break-up of AT&T and the creation of MCI which is a seven billion dollar a year corporation. He just died recently. He was instrumental in creating MCI Corporation that exists today and is prospering. Just think if Mr. McGowan who graduated from a local college here in Wilkes-Barre Pennsylvania, just think if he had gone to the moneyed interests and banks in our area who as I mentioned before were invested in AT&T and these other enterprises and said how about funding me with money so that I can fight AT&T. It's laughable because he just would not be in a position to obtain any money to do that kind of thing in our area. However outside of our area it's an entirely different story. In discussions I've had with Mr. McGowan prior to his death he had never indicated that he lacked self-esteem nor did he indicate that he had pursued the thought of overcoming AT&T by any different approach than going to Washington and finding sources of money in New York city and Washington to continue the fight against AT&T. While he was successful with the judge that finally made the ruling just think if he had tried to do that from the area of North Eastern Pennsylvania. How far do you think he would have gotten? Now another person who came from our area but did not actually experience the same kind of I want to call it trauma and that was Lee Iacocca who rose to great heights within the Ford and Chrysler Corporation, but we have to remember that while he may have come from the Bethlehem-Allentown area, those areas were completely distinct and completely different in both character and economic prosperity than the area just over the hill and up into North eastern Pennsylvania. It is like another world. However, I am giving him the benefit of the doubt that some of that may have rubbed off on him, but he did not let it come to him with the attitude of negativism and he moved out of the area and made something of himself. Others in our area moved out into the field of industrial enterprise and commercial enterprise and made a name for themselves I name among such people as and I will name them, but most of them did not realize why they could not make it in Wyoming Valley or North Eastern Pennsylvania. Those who made any kind of a living of any magnitude in our area made the good living because they were furthered by the moneyed interests and coal interests. While that was the prime reason that they were able to make any kind of success I do not want to take away from them their own native ability which would have to come into play even if money were given to them for an enterprise. I name among them, again I am not sure that these people how they got their money, but they certainly did get their money from the trust interests and that we'd more or less buy an idea that they were favored and that was Amedio Obici who founded the Planter's Peanut Corporation who later moved out of the area and down into the Virginia area. He started out on Wilkes Barre Public Square pedaling peanuts in a cart, roasted peanuts in a cart. Another one that I can Name is the original Andrew Sordoni who started out wheeling concrete and bricks through the Wilkes-Barre streets and Wyoming Valley streets and who became favored and invest- ment capital was provided to him and he succeeded in building Sordoni Construction Company, the Harvey's Lake Light Company, which later became part of the UGI Corporation in which the moneyed interest have tremendous investment. The Common Wealth Telephone Company which was also founded by him. Another person to my knowl- edge who was not an original founder, but was a native person was favored and took advantage of that favoritism and made something of himself Adams who put together what is now known as the Pennsylvania Enterprises is a scattering of different water companies and gas companies throughout the North Eastern part of Pennsylvania and he put them together to become what is now known as Pennsylvania Gas & Water and Pennsylvania Enterprises. One of the persons who was an heir to coal interests was John Dorrance II who's father left him approximately 120 million dollars and he squandered some forty mil- lion dollars before he decided to concentrate on the Campbell soup company that was left to him. However the main bulk of the money the eighty million dollars was made in the Dorrance Collieries in Wyoming Valley by his father and he went down into the Camden area where his father had created this soup company and decided to stay into the soup company and it is now known as the Campbell's Soup Company and that person John Dorrance till he died at the age of around seventy went to work every day. So he was very interested in his work, but he moved from the Wyoming Valley down to the Philadelphia area and set up his home down there. He became a billionaire, was written up in the Fortune magazine and never mentioned in the Fortune magazine that he ever came from North Eastern Pennsylvania and when he died there was an article in the Wall Street Journal detailing who his heirs were and his wife and his four children and they went into a long story of how he prospered in the soup company, but never mentioned that he ever was involved with the coal industry in North Eastern Pennsylvania nor did it mention in the article that any of his children ever had anything to do with the North Eastern part of Pennsylvania, Wilkes-Barre in particular, and yet the one person who now wants to, that's John Dorrance III, who has a ranch out in Wyoming of approximately thirty thousand acres by virtue of his inheritance from his father, who they claimed at one time sat on the pickle board part of the Campbell soup company, but didn't know what a pickle was, he is currently being castigated because he is trying to save tax money by abdicating his United States citizenship in order to evade taxes. Interesting to note that of all those that we have named and those who haven't been named which I will try to mention others, none of them have brought a great amount of industry or recommended a great amount of industry to North Eastern Pennsylvania, to my knowledge. Recently there was one gentleman who brought a number of jobs to the North Eastern part of Pennsylvania and that was Richard Stewart of the Traveler's Insurance Corporation who brought the Traveler's Medical Insurance Group to Nanticoke Pennsylvania he happens to be a Nanticoke native and his actual given name was Richard Starzinsky and it was noted that on the day that the dedication was made in the new enterprise he said I want to be known as Richard Starzinsky. It's interesting to note that outside of the Anthracite belt there are commercial enterprises some 20-60 miles north of Wilkes-Barre. In that areas there are such companies as the Sylvania Telephone Plant, the Charmin plant Procter & Gamble plant which produces children's diapers and bath tissue. The IBM facilities in Endicott and Johnson City and the IBM facility some eighty miles away (near) in Peekskill and the Philadelphia and Allentown areas which are only sixty to ninety miles away with not much out towards the western part of Pennsylvania. You don't get the people that were out of work in the coal fields to get opportunity there and the fact of the matter is that the ability for northeast people to get hired down that close to the coal production fields was difficult as compared to going a hundred miles away to New Jersey to the auto factories and the steel factories down United States Steel and Bethlehem steel thus it appears that the tougher jobs, the more difficult jobs were available to the people from North Eastern Pennsylvania if they moved down to those areas with the actual white collar work or blue collar work was non-existent as far as availability goes. People from the Wyoming Valley and Scranton area, and Schyllkill county area traveled as far as Ohio and Cleveland, Ohio and Detroit, Michigan, Chicago, Illinois to gain employment and again those jobs were, for the main part were in industrial operations or car factories. So it's interesting to note that while the moneyed interest and the coal interest grew and powered the industrial revolution and gave rise to the great enterprises none of this was served by the large majority of people in Northeastern Pennsylvania. As a matter of fact just to get a job as I mentioned was a difficult situation. Another interesting fact is that Connecticut which laid claim to all this ground upon which the anthracite coal was discovered and mined was one of the most highly concentrated machine tool manufacturers and industrial manufacturing enterprises in the United States Obviously the reason for that was the investment from their own people who controlled the coal and received the coal benefits was directed back to that state for the reason that as I mentioned earlier they would not want to bring those same enterprises from Connecticut into the coal producing areas for the reason that they would be challenging the workers to go from underground to above ground and obviously it wouldn't work. So the only manufacturing industries that really were relocated into the coal producing areas were something like the Vulcan Iron Works which provided parts and entire engines for the trains which were needed to haul the coal and then the hazard wire rope which was necessary, the cable was necessary for the mines to pull the cars out of the colliery out of the mines from the collieries so that they could be worked. So there was a tremendous need in mines for cable. So you can see the conclusions and lessons to be learned. So here we are in the coal producing areas and the

Northeastern Pennsylvania with a population of close to a million people where are we today in the area of employment, in the way, of skilled employment and high tech enterprises. We have very little of that. High tech enterprises only one or two companies, skilled kind of work, high paying work, very little. Average type of work tremendous amount of that but yet not enough to keep the employment level above the state of Pennsylvania average actually the unemployment rate above the Pennsylvania average and above the national average. So we can go forward with the idea that the people who are in positions of power will take the negatives that I have mentioned in the past shed those negatives and work towards positives too bring in high paying industries, skilled jobs and hopefully create a situation where the unemployment rate at some point and time will be less than the Pennsylvania rate and less than the national rate. The lesson we can learn from this is to improve our ability to become creative. Learn how to overcome obstacles, be more skilled in facing competition. As an example on how wealth is multiplied the original Dorranceton Methodist church in Kingston was built in 1897 on a lot one hundred by one hundred-thirty three feet which cost one thousand dollars and the building itself was built at the cost of two thousand dollar (see fig 15). That same building in 1995 which their celebrating its anniversary would cost close to a million dollars today. So you can imagine

That if these people as I go through the money angle and the trusts and how much was put into the trusts from the coal, you have to remember that two thousand dollars from 1897 if it were not disturbed and properly cared for would be worth a million dollars today. It's interesting to note from the Philadelphia Enquirer recent article current date 1995 indicated that Lee Bass from the Bass family of Texas who graduated from Yale in 1979 gave twenty million dollars and wanted it back because they would not follow his direction however, the whole family donated a total of eighty million to their alma mater. At Harvard A John. Lobe and his wife pledged seventy point five million one of the biggest donations in the history of America's higher education interesting that Lobe gave this money, this seventy point five million pledge and gave no restrictions on it. As we go through and study the coal trusts and their influence, direction, and power, and wealth it will be seen that these amounts of moneys that were given by these people are pale in comparison to the trusts that were developed and their value today and their influence throughout the economic spectrum and this is true because the trusts were set up properly and were not able to be broken by the heirs. In the case of Lobe and the case of the Bass family the heirs following through on that common management direction which will be indicated more fully later fall right in line with what the theory is that the first generation would make the money. The second generation would either make it or magnify it and the third generation will squander it. That was true in the case of the New York Central railroad and the Vanderbilt family. However in the coal trusts and the coal situations those were set up as English trusts so they have set these up so that the third, fourth, fifth, sixth generations with their lack of business knowledge or lack of business skills or lack of appetite for that kind of thing can not squander the money. So the money is doled out in certain amounts. One estimate is that five percent of the income and 5% of the principal is doled out to the trust participants on a yearly basis.

What the coal trusts received for their investment in Kirby is not known but I would guess that there's a substantial interest there in the Wool Worth Corporation and into the Kirby diversified interests and into the Allegheny Corporation and they were all public corporations and I would guess that some trust interest is in there. However it is very difficult to prove the exact interest because the trusts were individuals as well as cooperatives and they had to be careful that they were not attacked by the government as far as anti-trust goes. So they operated together, but yet they also operated alone and in most cases they operated alone and only when their interests were threatened and I will give you some examples of that would they vote together. So the period from

1920 to 1930 the coal interest trusts concentrated on investments in areas that had little or nothing to do with coal. Recognizing that the future was in steel, and oil, and gas, and in utilities. In the later part of 1920 to 1930 as you all know the great depression came about. There was a stock market crash and subsequent depression however in the North Eastern part of Pennsylvania that depression did not hit home because there was still quite a lot of coal production comparatively and so there were jobs available. There was no apple selling on the corners of the streets of North Eastern Pennsylvania. Aside from the coal industry there were other industries supported by these coal interests that weathered the stock market crash because their money was not as I mentioned before primarily invested in stocks it was invested in other things such as utilities etc. and they could weather that storm because they did not need to cash in their stock whatever ones they had and in many cases they were de facto owners of the enterprises in which they invested. In the period from 1930 to 1945 coal production continued to decline however there was still in every ton of coal there was fifty cents going to the trusts so there was a constant flow of cash into the trusts and a need to invest that. In the mean time they were majority owners the trusts were of the banking facilities in North Eastern Pennsylvania and while they could not be shown to be interlocking trusts they controlled the economy of North Eastern Pennsylvania and thereby controlled the chamber of commerce and controlled those who they would want to come into the area. Now between thirty and forty there was some interest in looking at the possibility of what the future might hold. And so there was loosening up on the tight control of keeping other competing industries out that would require labor, cheap labor, or abundant labor whichever you might describe it as. However with the unionism of the coal mines the miners began to get more benefits and better wages and so the miners had a decent living if they were working in the mines. While in the later part of thirty up near forty thirty nine as you know World War II began and with the Roosevelt administration there was an desire to provide the allies in Northern France with the weapons of war and so even though oil and gas were pushing to get a start there was a great need for coal still and so production continued in that period of time and into the World War II years to supply the military machine a matter of fact the low BTU gas did not go out of existence until approximately 1960.

The Kirby family by combining their Allegheny corporation with American Express created one of the largest financial corporations in the United States, so this was a family that possibly and we have no way of proving this copied the English trusts that were set up for the coal people and utilized the benefit of that kind of a trust to perpetuate the fortune. So they are one of the prime examples of a charitable endeavor that continues on and on and on and do not dissipate. Recently there's been some family infighting over the trust that gives away money to charity but to my knowledge the ownership of those interests that I mentioned is not in that challenge, it's strictly a name item type of thing that one of the brothers insisted that he has the right by his father to be the designator of the moneys from that one hundred and sixty-five million trust the interest portion the eight million dollars a year and the other brothers other parts of the family are fighting that brother's interest in doing so and to my knowledge it has not been resolved. It has been in the papers recently whether in fact the family is fighting over that kind of thing since they have such a grand name as benefactors to the North Eastern Pennsylvania. I hesitate to bring into the picture the current heirs of the many trusts that are still surviving from the hard coal anthracite days because many of them as in the Rockefeller family never really were interested or were able to pursue various ventures either by virtue of the fact that the lawyers who were set up to guard the trust who came from the families did not feel they had the capability or that they felt that the money would be better invested in the other areas and so while they received their share of the trust they never took hold and so there' very few names that you can pick out from the actual coal days except such as

John Dorrance who could show that they had the business acumen to take over the inheritance they had which for example John Dorrance inherited 120 million dollars and spent forty million of it before he decided to stay in the soup business that his father had originally built in Camden New Jersey the Campbell's Soup Company and he with his business acumen he carried that forward to the extent that he ran it up into a worth over a billion dollars and apparently the heirs as I mentioned the one specifically the one son are more or less having somewhat of a battle as to whether their inheritance of the shares of the Campbell's Soup Company ought to be sold or not. As I mentioned the one son who is trying to abdicate to did abdicate his citizenship in order to save taxes on his inheritance was not a real producer at the company as his father who went to work every day and most of the articles that I read do not think too highly of John Dorrance the third as to his contribution to the Campbell's Soup Company in fact they mentioned he was more interested in his ranch his thirty thousand acres of ranch out in Wyoming or out in the west there so it's not that easy to find people who inherited money from the trusts who actually took hold and multiplied outside of the trust multiplied the moneys into fabulous amounts with their endeavors. In a book entitled the Rich and the Super Rich by Lundberg published in the 1950's it was stated that he went through the various levels of income, how the income was distributed and from the study that he made he missed the entire wealth of North Eastern Pennsylvania that I mentioned because of these hidden trusts. He was not aware of where the actual wealth was at and in the 1920' and 1930' most of the millionaires in the United States were in the Northeastern Pennsylvania. Today according to the latest articles where a study has been made by IRS tax files on individuals there are approximately seventy thousand millionaires, however those seventy thousand millionaires while they may have an income of a million dollars shown on their return their actual net worth of many of the seventy thousand may be less than a million dollars because most of these people that report those kinds of income are on salaries with corporations and they live a lifestyle that consumes most of the money each year and so therefore they build no equitable amount of money and probably are not capable thinking wise to do so. So while for example many of the sports players income is beyond five, six million dollars a year, yet ten years later they have nothing because they are on a spending binge when they are earning that money and they have either poor advice on using the money themselves or poor advisors and so their actual net worth at the end of ten years in many cases is zero. Going back to the rail roads and Asa Packard who is the first person to benefit from the trusts to bring the rail roads into the North Eastern part of Pennsylvania to haul the coal to the major markets he was a benefactor of the again he was not a coal person he was picked by the coal trusts for his experience background or whatever and I have no way of actually finding out who actually said let's pick Asa Packard to bring the rail road in to the coal fields of northeastern Pennsylvania. In order for him to bring the rail road in they had to give him the ground they owned as I mentioned they owned all the ground so they had to give him the rights to the ground to bring the rail roads in to a certain area. So the coal benefited him but was not actually a coal inheritor. Now Asa Packard was the prime mover in developing up in Sayre Pennsylvania the Packard Hospital which is quite a well known hospital up there and an offshoot of that is the Guthrie Clinic which was named after one of the doctors up there who actually was married into a coal family in the Wyoming Valley and according to reports gave a donation of twelve million dollars to the Packard Hospital to establish the Guthrie Clinic now for a Doctor to in those days to earn or come by twelve million dollars is almost or more than impossible. So to determine how he came by that twelve million dollars to donated to the Packer Hospital is very difficult, but to speculate a little bit he was married into a very wealthy family who actually gave money to Robert Morris to give to George Washington to fight the Revolutionary War as one piece of knowledge and it's speculated that the twelve million actually came some way through that other family, by him marrying into that family. Just as we mentioned the story about Carpenter who again was sent down who was not a coal person was sent down to Dupont in the 1920' when they were in financial straits after World War I and then ended up marrying into the Dupont family but they took control of the Dupont Corporation with the coal money and ended up actually being the formative substance to bring to life the General Motors Corporation and they were caught in an anti-trust suit later and had to divest of the General Motors stock in order to satisfy the anti-trust people in the government. So until the days of the anti-trust actions which actually was precipitated by Rockefeller's rise to power but while I can not prove it I can speculate that Rockefeller, John D. Rockefeller was only an accountant in Ohio and as I mentioned before the wealth and land ability of the Connecticut claim extended into that area and the people apparently picked him to provide him with the funding to acquire and not taking away anything from John D. Rockefeller because he was not a coal person but he apparently was a very good businessman and got into the favor of these people and obtained the financing from them to do what he did which was to build the greatest oil empire in the history of the world. And it was the anti-trust legislation that came about that brought that situation down however even though it was divided into the number of companies the seven companies his power was still wielded throughout and again if you look at their family the money is still there to retrace Manhattan Bank, the Rockefeller Center which as an example of that the off shoot relatives or inheritors through trusts he was a little smarter than Commodore Vanderbuilt his trusts were set up almost and that's why I speculate that more than likely he was a beneficiary of the people from the coal because his trusts were set up in such a manner that the people that he left the money to could not over generations dissipate the wealth and Rockefeller center was left to heirs of the Rockefeller family and just recently they convinced the trusts to sell one half of the in recent years one half of their interest in the Rockefeller

Center to Japanese interests for a billion dollars. Interestingly enough one of the heirs a lady heir had said the reason that she pushed to sell one half the interest was because she was running out of money to donate to others.

To get out of that lack of self-esteem and replenish it is another matter, but interestingly enough there was a very famous and knowledgeable black person who wrote a book recently. He had made a study of slavery world wide and interestingly enough found that there were fourteen and a half million slaves taken from Africa by English interests Arab interests and other interests and other slave traders including black leaders in Africa and interestingly enough almost everyone I asked this question missed it by a great deal. Out of fourteen and a half million taken into slavery worldwide there were only 450,000 brought to the United States. That for use practical dissolution they were brought to the South and interestingly enough the reason they were brought to the south was to pick cotton, but since that time the 450,000 now are thirty-seven million people. There were more actual serfs in North Eastern Pennsylvania unknown serfs, unknowingly serving as serfs than there were black people brought into the U.S. The serfdom that I am speaking about was repeated in the south with some white people and in Arkansas and in other areas and in the south where they were share croppers, white share croppers, but not the kind of a system that was perpetuated in North Eastern Pennsylvania by the coal interests. So you might say if eliminate my premise is correct that the people were unknowingly treated as serfs who were brought in here to work the mines. The Welsh first then the Irish and then the European interests were brought in because of the coal since such a demand was being made for coal that they needed workers the coal interests sent agents over to Poland, to Russia, Hungary, Germany and etc....and paid bounties to agents who would bring individuals and families here to work in the mines. And interestingly enough I in fact since the slave trade was going on and there were actual workers who could be brought here from Africa who worked the mines why were not black people brought here? The simple answer to that is the people who received the Connecticut claim owned all of the ground and they by necessity were going to have to distribute that ground and so they brought their own kind of people here who were subservient as I mentioned the Welsh first because they were coal miners in England, then the Irish as the coal usage progressed and finally the European people to mine the coal. If you looked at the same category of people (immigrants) who went anywhere else in the United States, the number of people who achieved financial or business success percentage wise was much greater, particularly as the west was settled, than there were in the North Eastern part of Pennsylvania. The reason for that was that they the North East Pennsylvania people were mentally and physically and economically handicapped in that they were living in a controlled environment and the focus was on not on bringing people here to look for opportunity or be creative, their aim was exactly the opposite as they were looking for people who could do drudge work and were not interested in being creative. And be kept down economically and other ways! It was to their own self interest to keep that situation the way it was and so as the Welsh, Irish and others who could speak English later showed the ability to take advantage of certain businesses these people who controlled the banks and controlled the economies gave favors to those people, because they saw in them an opportunity to increase their wealth. So if it was a great big enterprise that would bring high wage industry into the area it was always frowned upon, and refused but not directly, indirectly it was denied and since there were no ways to keep from bring that information into the area, for example newspapers were controlled. There were very few ifs any colleges in the area until the late 1940's and early fifties. That was a hundred and fifty years after the coal already was depleted that now there was an impetus to further educate people in the area so that they could have more opportunity to go to school in the area. Prior to that the only people who were able to go to college were descendants of the coal interests who could afford to be sent out of the area, parents with the wherewithal to send their children out of the area would be small businessmen who were favored by the banks these owners who were picked out to be small time entrepreneurs and the beneficial interests or heirs of these trusts who by the very nature of their being they would want them to further their education in order to accept the responsibility. And so those people went to Yale, Harvard, Bucknell, other area schools outside of the coal district areas and then came back to the area to take positions of importance within their own organizations if they were capable of doing so and some went off into other areas, but by and large they came back into the area and took positions within the organization they had. As the coal depleted so did the opportunity for those second third and fourth generation heirs of the coal interests who themselves because now they were going up against much stiffer competition and now with the influx of the outside banks even though the trusts had actually turned their trusts over to these other banks and sold the local bank which they controlled and got into the larger bank with their influence they still carried some influence but basically it dissipated because now they were a small part of the large pie and so now the opportunity to be creative and the opportunity to expand within the next ten twenty and thirty years will be greatly enhanced in the North Eastern Part of Pennsylvania. From records at the courthouse it can be determined that there are still many of the trusts who dissipate each year a large amount of money to the managers of the trust and to the beneficiaries of the trust. For example, it's well known that there are more than twenty five and more trusts where the people who are the managers and these are mostly lawyers receive compensation from the trust in the form of a management fee of $250,000-$500,000 strictly for being the manager of the trust and these people in general are third, fourth, and fifth generation people descendants of the original Connecticut claim. If you compare this with the rich and the super rich and the information in there by Lundberg which indicated that of the people in the United States who possess wealth and this was in 1950 there were somewhat like 2,000 millionaires in the United States in 1950. Today as I mentioned before there are stated 70,000 millionaires. In 1950 that amounted to less than one percent of the total people in the United States that had the million dollars, a tenth of one percent. And in 1995 the even if you considered that the seventy thousand were actual millionaires by net worth it's a very small tiny percentage, but if you analyze what I said in this small part of the United States in the North Eastern part of Pennsylvania and if you extrapolate the trusts. And if you extrapolate this information and take the area of North Eastern Pennsylvania as compared to the area of the United States there is still to this day this is a tremendous concentration of wealth here and wealth and wealth means power. For example North Eastern Pennsylvania is 7th in the nation in personal assets which include certificates of deposit, saving accounts, stocks, bonds, cash, and U. S. savings bonds. . While the trusts are still operating and have tremendous power if banded together, The exercise there of is limited because by law in the laws of today if the trusts were to operate together they would be in violation of the anti-trust laws and this they would try to avoid. However in one recent situation within the last ten years it was noted that when there was a challenge to some power in one of the companies in which the trusts are invested heavily. To stave off a challenge, they had to vote by personally appearing five lawyers came to the meeting and voted seventy-three percent of the shares of this publicly traded corporation. So that this showed you that they were by law allowed to vote together yet by anti-trust laws this was illegal and if this concentration of economic power were able to be banded together, which it is not, as I mentioned and is actually or secretively controlled and in some situations competitively controlled, but if it were able to be banded together and voted as it was a hundred years ago, a hundred years ago there was no worry about voting together, so they could do what I'm speculating about today, but they can not do because of the anti-trust laws they could do with impunity and therefore their control across the country in that frame of time was practically unlimited as compared to today, their control is minimal collectively however individually they have some power, but it's hard to determine where that power lies. For example in the sell out of the various banks in North Eastern Pennsylvania to the major banks it's impossible to determine who is in charge of the new bank. One bank president that I talked to who actually ran the bank for years never knew that the trusts were the controlling interests in the bank and even challenged me on that until I showed him how the trusts were detailed with their shares and how they were not voted by the individuals, but voted by the trusts. So while the individual names showed in the corporation's shares and distribution those people could not actually vote those shares it was the trustee who was the lawyer who controlled the trust who voted those shares and so the five lawyers may have controlled two hundred names or five hundred names whatever the case may be and voted those shares collectively for the bank. When that was necessitated. I was amazed that the president working in the bank was not aware of who the owners and controllers of the bank were. I found out that sometime later that the person was not really privy to what was going on with the trusts as he was as many were chosen by the trusts to be one of the people who they favored and who would be loyal to the interests of the trusts. So when the banks were sold out a lot of the power of the trusts individually and collectively was lost and that is why I say that within the next ten to thirty years there will be a great increase of self-esteem and creativity and in actual expansion of the economic sphere within our area. This does not say that the trusts will disappear nor will their economic power disappear because as I mentioned collectively they have power without action and that may happen again and it may be challenged if it ever does happen it may be challenged that the trusts would have to exert their power collectively to dominate a particular situation. Such as they did with the Dupont situation as I mentioned before and the backing of someone like Kirby and some other names, Rockefeller as I mentioned, and to my knowledge Vanderbuilt himself was a pawn of the J. P. Morgan interests who were actually controlled by the interests in North Eastern Pennsylvania to control the New York Central Rail Road, because that was a conduit to move the anthracite coal within the New York, Philadelphia, and other areas and the same with the Union Pacific that was a way of investing their money to further their own interests for moving the steel and moving the coal to other markets and to this day the Union Pacific is controlled out of Bethlehem Pennsylvania and if it were to be examined, more than likely controlled by the trusts, in North Eastern Pennsylvania who have the greatest share. Another example is the St. Joe Paper Company which has the Beelin family which owns one thirtieth of the Florida land and has a great charitable interest 5 billion within it that was another one I mentioned, but that's a real coal interest from the old line Beelin and Wells family and today the St. Joe Company itself I am sure through these trusts has a lot of power within that company the power to dictate who the directors are, who the controllers of the trusts are. There were recently some articles in the paper detailing out some infighting among the St. Joe people as to how the charitable money should be distributed and it's been resolved recently by some internal agreements, but as far as how much of the St. Joe's stock is controlled by these trusts is difficult to determine because as I said the trusts by their very nature are secretive instruments and there is no liability or desire of those who have trusts to disclose the inner workings of those trusts. One small item which actually is a big item, but it takes away the focus of what the total book is and that is to show that the coal was the instrument by which the people were manipulated and enslaved and the loss of that coal or decline of that coal and the emergence of oil brought about the freedom of the people and the emergence of new and different economic powers and so I want to try to emphasize that this is a story not of North Eastern Pennsylvania because that again turns people off, but the story of what happened in North Eastern Pennsylvania and it happened without the people realizing what happened and to this day unless they read this book will not know what happened to them. So many people from northeast Pennsylvania died never knowing that they were manipulated into a certain situation nor do I say that this was a bad thing to be done because I would not be here for example had it not been for the fact that my father and mother immigrated here to be in the coal fields of northeastern Pennsylvania. And interestingly enough the coal fields were dominated by the people that I mentioned and were brought here and actually put into serfdom by the people who had the coal interest, but they could not convince the Arab population nor the Jewish population to go into the mines. Those people became entrepreners and shied away from the mines except for a very few. Most stayed away from working in the mines s in producing the coal because they were denied either by their intelligence or lack of thereof they were denied the opportunity to get good jobs with the coal interests so they ended up as beneficiaries of the coal interests as entrepreneurs and were financed in those ventures through the small businesses that they got into.

In the local newspaper recently there was a breakdown of the population and the household income and education characteristics in our area of northeastern Pennsylvania, This is ninety-five years after nineteen hundred and another hundred and ninety-five years from the time that coal was first discovered in the area, basically the area is still lacking in manufacturing capability which is desperately needed and this drags down the household and median income individuals and households and actually by having these characteristics against you it still causes you to lose your most creative and inventive people to other areas. And so what we have to do is turn this around by bringing in more manufacturing and more creative type entrepreneurial businesses that can generate jobs and income. Recently I discovered another important and interesting fact that the Chemung County of New York which the largest city is Elmira which was settled by and developed by people from the Wyoming Valley area and this is interesting because having known the Chemung County area to be heavy in manufacturing it's understandable that these people from here took the coal money and in order not to take away the labor from the coal mines set up manufacturing industries up in the Elmira area, including such industries as Westinghouse, General Electric, Remington-Rand, those kinds of manufacturing Kennedy Valve number of other manufacturing operations. The blue print for the future of Luzerne County and North Eastern Pennsylvania would read like this it would be necessary to raise the manufacturing component and that could include all different kinds of manufacturing not necessarily steel making or auto making but any kind of manufacturing that would create jobs that would bring wages up to the level that's comparable to some of the surrounding states and other areas of Pennsylvania so that the tangible individual income and household income and median could rise to their level. This is not something that is easy to accomplish or can be done over night, but there is a movement by the Chambers of Commerce in our area to go after these kinds of jobs in a more critical fashion and they are more or less unimpeded at this time because of the lack of control that existed in the early mining days. In the early economic area when the banks were controlled by either mining interests or their trusts, while they did not vote together they did when the time came to do so especially when their interests were being threatened .So the advent of the interstate banking system has been a godsend to North Eastern Pennsylvania because it now allows the bigger banks to come in and analyze a project basically on what's good for the bank, what's good for the area, and what's good for the individual proposing the business proposition. This is interesting because in the early days this could not be done, for the proposition's were never acted upon if it had any threat to impinging on the coal mine labor force. So the advent of interstate banking is a positive thing. One of the negative factors which was a nationwide situation was the 1989 enactment of the Fierra, or new banking law which after a struggle including a bail out of the savings and loans to the present time in 1999 has resulted in a situation that the even the interstate banks (the large banks) are not looking for risk loans and so what they are doing is primarily investing their funds (which they get from the depositors) and their earnings and trust funds in so called safe havens such as treasury certificates, home loans, home equity lines of credit places where they could recover their money fast if there is a threat of a loss or if there is a loss it is a minuscule loss compared to millions of dollars invested in some one small business or larger business enterprise. And so the basic equity money and venture money that's being obtained and regular capital formation money is actually being obtained through subsidiary operations like GE Capital, IT&T, Westinghouse, Greyhound, and other types of financing entities however a number of them have recombined together or merged together or have some have even gone out of business because of the more risky they were handling the more risky types of situations, but the capital is available through these sources and Hopefully the people of North Eastern Pennsylvania will come upon the knowledge that this is available and that they will take advantage of the situation.

Another thing that would be necessary to implement a long range goal of raising the household income and individual income in North Eastern Pennsylvania would be to create within the college both community college, and four year college and university in our North Eastern part of Pennsylvania create more seminars, courses, etc....on creativity, entrepreneurship and how to start a business. This is very important to keep people who have the native intelligence here and who have the ability to start a business to keep them here and provide them with the tools that is the capital to implement that particular idea. The state has tried to so this on a statewide level, but you have to remember that they are competing in the whole state of Pennsylvania and while the federal government has some programs they are not of prime importance to solving North Eastern Pennsylvania's problem. So we have to look within our own back yard and dig up all of the sources we have, risk capital situations should be encouraged and organized and by having this available at least there would be places that people with creative ideas can come to, to have them analyzed searched out and assisted in bringing them to fruition if they are good ideas through using creative problem solving methods. This is very important for the future if we are to grow economically and provide good jobs good opportunities and good income for our children and our grand children and future children and grand children. The time to start is now, the impediments have been reduced if not eliminated and we can not afford to wait we have to move forward and try to implement the procedures, practices and proven methods that have worked in other areas of the country. Remember that we have been unique. We have been in a situation for more than a hundred and fifty years where the economics have been controlled by a small group of individuals who had their own self-interest at heart and so we have to now forget about that and we have to remember that was an impediment, but it should not be an impediment to the future. We are in a race for the future in competition with others throughout Pennsylvania and throughout the United States. We can learn from those who have succeeded. We can copy and implement those tools that have worked for them. The main thing to remember is that we are equal to them. Our esteem is greater now than it has ever been and we must begin to look at ourselves as people able and willing to succeed. And that success will come to us. Maybe we won't win the race because we have been so far behind, but we can get closer to the finish line. As we look at our past let us not look at it with a negative attitude that it's a reason for where we are, but let's look on it as a situation that over which we or are parents, or grand parents had no control or knowledge of. We now have the knowledge, we now have the ability to move forward and we don't have anyone around us who can control us because of the reasons I mentioned before. So whatever progress we make from here on in will be because of our own doing and will be to our own credit. We can not look on the past as a self pity tool we have to look on it as a part of the blue print for the future or as I have said if we can know what the past has been then we can not or should not make the same mistakes in the future, but we can use that past to pave our way into the future.

Wage statistics for the period 1801 to 1933 in the United States

In 1801 the average worker made $9.30 for a six-day workweek or $483.60 per year. In 1818 the wage rose to $1.90 per day or $11.46 per workweek or $595.92 per year. In 1830 the average wage fell back to $1.73 per day or $10.38 per workweek or $539.76 per year. In 1860 the average skilled worker wage was $9.72 for a six-day week or slightly more than the 1801 wages the daily wage was $1.62 and $505.46 per year. These included carpenters, engineers, and machinists. This wage was then also a comparable wage paid to a miner in North Eastern Pennsylvania. In 1879 an average skilled laborer in manufacturing made $2.26 per day or $13.56 per six day week or $705.12 per year (a miner made $300 a year). In 1900 a person working in finance, insurance or real estate made $1,040.00 per year or $20.00 per week or $3.33 per day in a six-day week. In 1902 miners made $2.75 per day, laborers .18 cents per hour and Breaker Boys made .13 cents per hour and mule driven .13 cents and hour, tracklayers .24 cents per hour, children slate pickers got .06 cents an hour. In 1921 the peak year of anthracite production the average worker in finance, insurance, or real estate was earning an average of $1,860 a year or $37.56 per week or $5.96 per day. In 1933 the same workers made less an average of $1,555 a year or $29.90 per week or $4.98 per day.

Ref: Money Supply in 1830's and 1997.

1999 comparison of hard currency (cash) and liquid assets in U.S.

At the end of 1997 there was available 426 billion worth of hard U.S. currency (cash) in circulation worldwide.

Americans alone had 6.6 trillion of savings account, certificates of deposit, money market funds, and other similar liquid assets. In addition Americans had 13 trillion worth of stocks and 3.3 trillion worth of corporate bonds. In addition liquid assets such as real estate would put a tremendous strain on the limited green back supply. The ratio being that demand exceeded supply by some 40 to 1. Therefore this kind of run on banks could cause a panic such as in 1837 when a major economic depression resulted from speculation in inflated land values and caused more than 800 banks to suspend currency payments to customers. More then 600 financial institutions failed that year of 1837.

FIG 1—THE PUJO REPORT

FIGURE 1—THE FINAL REPORT OF THE PUJO COMMITTEE

FINAL REPORT FROM THE PUJO COMMITTEE, FEBRUARY 28, 1913

The firm members and directors whose affiliations are shown number 180. In the aggregate they hold 385 directorships in 41 banks and trust companies having total resources of $3,832,000,000 and total deposits of 12,834,000,000; 50 directorships in 11 insurance companies having total assets of $2,646,000,000; 155 directorships in 31 railroad systems having a total capitalization of $12,193,000,000 and a total mileage of 163,200; 6 directorships in 2 express companies and 4 directorships in 1 steamship company with a combines capital of $245,000,000 and a gross income of #97,000,000; 98 directorships in 28 producing and trading corporations having a total capitalization of $3,583,000,000 and a total gross annual earnings in excess of $1,145,000,000; and 48 directorships in 19 public utility corporations having a total capitalization of $2,826,000,000 and total gross annual earnings in excess of $428,000,000; in all, 746 directorships in 134 corporations having total resources or capitalization of $25,325,000,000.

J.P. Morgan & Co. of New York (identical with Drexel & Co. of Philadelphia) having 23 directorships in 13 banks and trust companies, namely:

New York:

Astor Trust............

.3

Bankers' Trust ....

3

Chemical National Bank............

..2

First National Bank............

..3

Guaranty Trust Co............

3

Liberty National Bank............

..1

National Bank of Commerce............

2

National City Bank............

1

New York Trust Co............

..1

Philadelphia:

Fourth Street National Bank............

..1

Franklin National Bank............

..1

Girard Trust Co............

.1

Philadelphia National Bank............

1

having total resources of $1,406,000,000 and total deposits of $989,000,000.

Four directorships in 4 insurance companies, namely:

Fidelity & Casualty Co............

.1

German-American Insurance Co............

..1

Mutual Life Insurance Co............

.1

Penn Mutual Life Insurance Co............

1

and a controlling stock interest in another, the Equitable Life Assurance Society of New York, having total assets of $1,249,000,000.

Twenty directorships in 12 transportation systems, namely:

International Mercantile Marine............

3

Adams Express Co............

1

Atchison, Topeka, & Santa Fe............

..1

Chicago Great Western............

.1

Erie

3

Lehigh Valley............

2

New York Central & Hudson River............

.1

New York, New Haven & Hartford............

.1

Northern Pacific............

3

Pere Marquette............

..2

Reading Co............

1

Southern.........

1

having a total capitalization of $4,379,000,000 and a total mileage of 48,000 for the railroads and gross income of $72,000,000 for the express and steamship companies.

Twelve Directorships in 7 producing and trading corporations, namely;

Baldwin Locomotive Works............

.1

General Electric Co............

..2

International Agriculture Corporation............

..1

International Harvester Co............

..2

Pullman Co............

1

United States Steel Corporation............
..4
Westinghouse Electric & Manufacturing Co............
1

having a total capitalization of $1,989,000,000 and total gross annual earnings in excess of $899,000,000.

Four Directorships in 3 public utility corporations, namely:
American Telephone & Telegraph Co............
..1
Philadelphia Rapid Transit Co............
..2
Public Service Corporation of New Jersey............
..1

having a total capitalization of $1,013,000,000 and total gross annual earnings of $234,000,000.

In all, 63 directorships in 39 corporations having total resources or capitalization of $10,036,000,000.

J.P. Morgan & Co. have 2 of the 3 voting trustees of the Guaranty Trust Co. of New York and 1 of the three voting trustees of the Bankers trust Co. of New York (2 until George W. Perkins retied from Morgan & Co. and was succeeded as one of the such trustees by an attorney of the trust company); 1 of the 3 voting trustees of the Chicago Great Western; 2 of the 5 voting trustees of the International Mercantile Marine Co.; 1 of the 3 voting trustees of the Southern; 1 of the 5 voting trustees of the International Agricultural Corporation; 1 each of the voting trustees in the expired voting trusts of the stock International Harvester Co., Northern Pacific, Reading Co., and Erie RR

FIRST NATIONAL BANK OF NEW YORK

The First National Bank of New York has 33 directorships in 14 banks and trust companies, namely:

New York:

United States Trust Co............

1

New York Trust CO............

.3

National Bank of Commerce............

3

Liberty National Bank............

..2

Hanover National Bank............

1

Guaranty Trust Co. ....

.3

Farmers' Loan & Trust Co............

..1

Chemical National Bank ....

.1

Chase National Bank............

5

Bankers Trust Co............

.5

Astor Trust Co............

.4

Chicago:

Illinois Trust & Savings Bank............

..2

First Trust & Savings Bank............

..1

First National Bank............

..1

having total resources of $1,557,000,000 and total deposits of $1,181,000,000.

having total resources of $2,435,000,000 and total gross annual earnings in excess of $1,020,000,000.

Five Directorships in 3 public utility corporations, namely:

American Telephone & Telegraph Co............

.3

Commonwealth Edison Co............

..1

Consolidated Gas Co............

1

having a total capitalization of $891,000,000 and total gross earnings of $242,000,000.

In all, 89 directorships in 49 corporations having total assets or capitalization of $11,393,000,000.

The First National Bank of New York had 1 of 5 voting trustees of the International Agriculture Corporation, 1 of 5 voting trustees of the International Mercantile Marine Co., 2 of the 3 voting trustees of the Chicago Great Western, 2 of the 3 voting trustees of the Southern, 1 of the 3 voting trustees of the Bankers Trust Co., 2 of the 3 voting trustees of the Guaranty Trust Co. Also 1 each of the voting trustees in the expired voting trusts of the stock of Erie, Reading Co., Northern Pacific, and St. Louis & San Francisco.

GUARANTY TRUST CO. OF NEW YORK

The Guaranty Trust co. of New York has 63 directorships in 19 banks and trust companies, namely:

New York:

United States Mortgage & Trust Co............

1

United States Trust Co............

.1

Union Trust Co............

.1

National City Bank............

1

National Bank of Commerce............

12

Mechanics & Metals National Bank............

..4

Liberty National Bank............

5

First National Bank............

3

Farmers Loan & Trust Co............

.2

Equitable Trust Co............

1

Chemical National Bank............

4

Chase National Bank............

.2

Central Trust Co............

1

Bankers Trust Co............

..9

Astor Trust Co............

.11

American Exchange National Bank............

1

Five directorships in 5 insurance companies, namely:
New York Life Insurance Co............

1

Mutual Life Insurance Co............

.1

Equitable Life Assurance Society............
.1
Continental Insurance Co............
.1
American Surety Co............
.1

having total resources of $1,819,000,000.
Twenty-six directorships in 12 railroad systems, namely:
Southern............
2
Seaboard Air Line............
.1
Reading Co............
1
Northern Pacific............
.4
New York, New Haven & Hartford............
..2
New York Central & Hudson River............
..2
Lehigh Valley............
.2
Great Northern............
..1
Erie...
1
Delaware, Lackawanna & Western............
4
Rock Island Co. and Chicago, Rock Island & Pacific Railway............
..4

Chicago, Burlington & Quincy............

..2

having total resources of $4,643,000,000 and mileage of 61,400.

One director in 1 express company, namely, Adams Express Co. having total resources of $48,000,000 and gross income of $33,000,000.

Nineteen directorships in 13 producing and trading corporations, namely:

Westinghouse Electric & Manufacturing Co............

1

United States Steel Corporation............

..3

United States Rubber Co............

..1

Pullman Co............

..3

National Biscuit Co............

.2

Lackawanna Steel Co............

..1

International Harvester Co............

..1

International Agricultural Corporation............

1

General Electric Co............

.1

Baldwin Locomotive Works............

1

American Car & Foundry Co............

..1

American Can Co............

.2

American Agricultural Chemical Co............

1

having a total capitalization of $910,000,000 and total gross annual earnings of $302,000,000.

In all, a total of 160 directorships in 76 companies having total assets or capitalization of $17,342,000,000.

In addition, the Guaranty Trust Co. has voting trustee each in the voting trusts for stock of the Interborough Metropolitan Co., International Agricultural Corporation, International Nickel Co., Chicago Great Western, Southern Railway, and 2 voting trustees each in voting trusts of Intercontinental Rubber Co. and Bankers Trust Co.

BANKER'S TRUST CO. OF NEW YORK

The Bankers' Trust Co. of New York have 59 directorships in 19 banks and trust companies, namely:

Illinois Trust & Savings Bank, Chicago............

1

Fourth National Bank, Philadelphia............

..1

Franklin National Bank, Philadelphia............

1

Girard Trust Co., Philadelphia............

..1

Astor Trust Co., New York............

.14

Bank of Manhattan Co., New York............

.1

Chase National Bank, New York............

.3

Chemical National Bank, New York............

3

Corn Exchange Bank, New York............
.1
Equitable Trust Co., New York............
1
First National Bank, New York............
5
Fourth National Bank, New York............
1
Guaranty Trust Co., New York............
9
Hanover National Trust, New York............
.1
Liberty National Bank, New York............
.7
Mechanics & Metals National Bank, New York............
2
National Bank of Commerce, New York............
4
National Park Bank, New York............
..1
United States Mortgage and Trust Co., New York............
.2

having total resources of $1,754,000,000 and total deposits of $1,229,000,000.

Ten directorships in 7 insurance companies, namely:
American Surety Co., New York............
.3
Continental Insurance Co............
.1
Equitable Life Assurance Society............
.2

Chicago Great Western............
1
Chicago, Burlington & Quincy............
.1
Baltimore & Ohio............
.1
Atchison, Topeka & Santa Fe............
.....3

having a total capitalization of $10,241,000,000 and a total mileage of 131,200.

Two directorships in 2 express companies, namely:
Wells Fargo & Co............
.1
Adams Express Co............
1

having a total capitalization of $72,000,000 and gross annual earnings of $58,000,000.

Twenty-four directorships in 16 producing and trading companies, namely:
Westinghouse Electric & Manufacturing Co............
.2
United States Steel Corporation............
3
Pullman Co............
1
Lackawanna Steel Co............
1
International Paper Co............
..1

International Nickel Co............
.1
International Harvester Co............
1
International Agricultural Corporation............
..3
Intercontinental Rubber Co............
..2
Colorado Fuel & Iron Co............
.1
Baldwin Locomotive Works............
.2
American Sugar Refining Co............
1
American Smelting & Refining Co............
1
American Locomotive Co............
.1
American Can Co............
..2
Amalgamated Copper Co............
..1

having a total capitalization of $2,757,000,000 and total gross annual earnings of $963,000,000.

Eight directorships in 6 public utilities corporations, namely:
Philadelphia Co............
1
New York Railways Co............
2
International Traction Co............
.1

Interboro Metropolitan & Interboro Rapid Transit Co............
1
Consolidated Gas Co............
1
American Telegraph & Telephone Co............
..2
Fidelity & Casualty Co............
..1
Mutual Life Insurance Co............
1
New York Life Insurance Co............
..1
Northwestern Mutual Life Insurance Co............
.1

having total assets of $2,119,000,000.
Fifteen directorships in 11 transportation systems, namely:
Atchison, Topeka, & Santa Fe............
1
Chicago & Great Western............
..1
Chicago, Rock Island & Pacific Railway. & Rock Island Co............
..3
Denver & Rio Grande............
.1
Lehigh Valley............
..1
Missouri Pacific............
..1
New York, New Haven & Hartford............
1
Northern Pacific............
..1

Pennsylvania............

2

Pere Marquette............

1

Seaboard Air Line............

2

having a total capitalization of $4,231,000,000 and a total mileage of 55,000.

Twenty-three directorships in 13 producing and trading companies, namely:

American Agricultural Chemical Co............

..1

American Beet Sugar Co............

1

American Can Co............

..3

American Car & Foundry Co............

.1

American Locomotive Co............

..1

Baldwin Locomotive Works............

..3

International Agricultural Corporation............

3

International Nickel Co............

..2

International Paper Co............

2

National Biscuit Co............

.1

United States Rubber Co............
.1
United States Steel Co............
2
Westinghouse Electric & Manufacturing Co............
..2

having a total capitalization of $2,150,000,000 and total gross annual earnings of $840,000,000.

Six directorships in 5 public utility corporations, namely:

having a total capitalization of $394,000,000, and a total gross annual earnings of $72,000,000.

In all, 86 directors in 47 corporations with total resources of capitalization of $13,205,000,000.

The National City Bank also had 1 voting trustee in the voting trust of the stock of the International Harvester Co., which has expired.

KUHN, LOEB & CO.

Kuhn, Loeb & Co., of New York, have seven directorships in six banks and trust companies, namely:

Central Trust Co., New York............
1
Equitable Trust, New York............
.1
Fourth National Bank, New York............
1
National Bank of Commerce, New York............
1
National City Bank, New York............
1
United States Mortgage & Trust Co., New York............
2

having a total capitalization of $810,000,000 and total gross annual earnings of $530,000,000.

One directorship in one insurance company, namely, American Surety Co., having total assets of $8,000,000.

Five directorships in 3 railroad systems, namely:

Baltimore & Ohio............

..1

Southern Pacific............

2

Union Pacific............

.2

having a total mileage of 21,000 and total capitalization of $2,101,000,000.

One directorship in 1 express company, namely, Wells, Fargo & Co., having a total capitalization of $24,000,000 and total gross annual earnings of $25,000,000.

One directorship in one producing and trading company, namely, Westinghouse Electric & Manufacturing Co., having a total capitalization of $68,000,000 and a gross income of $34,000,000.

In all, 15 directorships in 12 corporations with total assets or capitalization of $3,011,000,000.

Atchison, Topeka & Santa Fe............

..1

Baltimore & Ohio............

.1

Chesapeake & Ohio............

..1

Chicago, Milwaukee & St. Paul............

3

Chicago & Northwestern............
.3
Delaware, Lackawanna & Western............
..5
Illinois Central............
..1
Missouri, Kansas & Texas............
1
New York Central & Hudson River............
.2
New York, New Haven & Hartford............
.1
Norfolk & Western............
..1
Northern Pacific............
1
Pennsylvania............
.1
Reading Co............
1
Seaboard Air Line............
.1
Southern Pacific............
2
Union Pacific............
.2

having a total capitalization of $8,308,000,000 and a total mileage of 100,400.

One director in 1 steamship company, namely, International Mercantile Marine, having a total capitalization of $173,000,000 and total gross annual earnings of $39,000,000.

Fifteen directorships in 9 producing and trading companies, namely:

Amalgamated Copper Co............
..1

American Sugar Refining Co............
.2

Armour & Co............
.2

Baldwin Locomotive Works............
..1

Central Leather Co............
.1

Inter-Continental Rubber Co............
1

International Harvester............
.1

Lackawanna Steel............
.4

United States Steel Corp............
..2

having a total capitalization of $2,211,000,000, and total gross annual earnings in excess of $812,000,000.

Nine directors in 3 public utilities companies, namely:

Chicago Elevated Railways............
.2

Consolidated Gas Co............
..6

New York Railways............
1

NATIONAL BANK OF COMMERCE OF NEW YORK

The National Bank of Commerce of New York has 57 directorships in 22 banks and trust companies, namely:

Illinois Trust & Savings Bank, Chicago............ .1

Merchants Loan & Trust Co., Chicago............ ..1

Girard Trust Co., Philadelphia............ 1

Mellon National Bank, Pittsburgh............ ..1

Union Trust Co., Pittsburgh............ 1

American Security & Trust Co., Washington............ .1

Astor Trust Co., New York............ 6

Bankers' Trust Co., New York............ ..4

Central Trust Co., New York............ .4

Chase National Bank, New York............ 3

Chemical National Bank, New York............ ..2

Equitable Trust Co., New York............ ..4

Farmers Loan & Trust Co., New York............ 3

First National Bank, New York............ ..3

Guaranty Trust Co., New York............
.12
Liberty National Bank, New York............
..3
Mechanics & Metals National Bank, New York............
.1
National City Bank, New York............
2
United States Mortgage & Trust Co., New York............
1
United States Trust Co., New York............
.1

having total resources of $2,110,000,000 and total deposits of $1,567,000,000.

Twenty-one directorships in 9 insurance companies, namely:

American Surety Co............
8
Continental Insurance Co............
1
Equitable Life Assurance Society............
3
German-American Insurance Co............
.1
Home Insurance Co............
.1
Metropolitan Life Insurance Co............
..1
Mutual Life Insurance Co............
4
New York Life Insurance Co............
..1

Northwestern Mutual Life Insurance Co............
.1
American Light & Traction Co............
1
American Telephone & Telegraph Co............
.2
International Traction Co., Buffalo............
.1
Philadelphia Co., Pittsburgh............
..1
United Gas Improvement Co., Philadelphia............
..1

having a total capitalization of $930,000,000 and total gross annual earnings of $205,000,000.

In all, the Bankers' Trust Co. of New York has 113 directorships in 55 companies, having a total capitalization of resources of $11,184,000,000.

The Bankers' Trust Co. have 1 voting trustee each in the voting trusts of stock in the International Agricultural Corporation and International Nickel Co., and 2 voting trustees each in the voting trusts of stock of the Intercontinental Rubber Co. and Guaranty Trust Co.

NATIONAL CITY BANK OF NEW YORK

The National City Bank of New York has 32 directorships in 16 banks and trust companies, namely:
Central Trust Co., Chicago............
.1
Continental & Commercial National Bank, Chicago ....
.3
Continental & Commercial Trust & Savings Bank, Chicago............
.1

Merchants Loan & Trust Co., Chicago............
..1
Mellon National Bank, Pittsburgh............
..1
Union Trust Co., Pittsburgh............
1
American Security & Trust Co., Washington............
.1
Riggs National Bank, Washington............
..1
Bank of Manhattan Co., New York............
1
Central Trust Co., New York............
.1
Farmers Loan & Trust Co., New York............
..9
Guaranty Trust Co., New York............
..1
Hanover National Bank, New York............
1
National Bank of Commerce, New York............
3
New York Trust Co., New York............
3
United States Trust Co., New York............
3

having total resources of $1,532,000,000 and total deposits of $1,130,000,000.

One director in 1 insurance company, namely, Mutual Life Insurance Co. of New York, having total assets of $587,000,000.

Twenty-eight directorships in 17 railroad companies, namely: having total assets of $2,509,000,000.

Thirty-six directorships in 23 railroad systems, namely:

Atchison, Topeka & Santa Fe...........

.2

Baltimore & Ohio...........

1

Chesapeake & Ohio...........

.1

Chicago, Burlington & Quincy...........

.1

Chicago, Rock Island & Pacific & Rock Island Co...........

.1

Delaware & Hudson...........

.1

Delaware, Lackawanna & Western...........

..1

Denver & Rio Grande...........

..1

Erie...

2

Illinois Central...........

..3

Lehigh Valley...........

1

Missouri, Kansas & Texas...........

.1

Missouri Pacific...........

.1

New York Central & Hudson River...........

..1

New York, New Haven & Hartford............
..1
Norfolk & Western............
1
Northern Pacific............
.1
Reading Co............
.2
Seaboard Air Line............
..2
Southern Pacific............
.3
Southern Railway............
..2
Union Pacific............
.3
Wabash......
..3

having total capitalization of $8,901,000,000 and total mileage of 111,200.

One directorship in 1 steamship company, the International Mercantile Marine, having total capitalization of $173,000,000 and total gross income of $39,000,000.

Four directorships in 2 express companies, namely:
Wells-Fargo & Co............
1
Adams Express Co............
3

Twenty directorships in 17 producing and trading companies, namely:

American Can Co............
.1
American Locomotive Co............
.1
American Smelting & Refining Co............
1
Amalgamated Copper............
1
United Shoe Machinery Corporation............
2
Virginia-Carolina Chemical Co............
.1

having a capitalization of $298,000,000 and total gross annual earnings in excess of $39,000,000.

Three directorships in three public utility companies, namely:
Brooklyn Rapid Transit............
1
Consolidated Gas............
.1
Philadelphia Rapid Transit Co............
.1

having a capitalization of $479,000,000 and total gross annual earnings of $97,000,000. Grand total, 37 directorships in 29 corporations with total assets or capitalization of $7,495,000,000.

CHASE NATIONAL BANK OF NEW YORK

The Chase National Bank of New York have 22 directorships in 10 banks and trusts companies, namely:
First National Bank of Chicago............
..1

Illinois Trust & Savings Bank of Chicago............
..1
Bankers Trust Co. of New York............
3
Farmers Loan & Trust Co., New York............
..1
Guaranty Trust Co. of New York............
..2
First Trust & Savings Bank of Chicago............
.1
Astor Trust Co. of New York............
3
First National Bank of New York............
..5
Liberty National Bank of New York............
2
National Bank of Commerce of New York............
.3

having total resources of $1,275,000,000 and total deposits of $987,000,000.

Seven directorships in 5 insurance companies, namely:
American Surety Co............
3
Continental Insurance Co............
1
Mutual Life Insurance Co............
1
New York Life Insurance Co............
..1
Northwestern Mutual Life Insurance Co............
.1

having total assets of $1,605,000,000.

Seventeen directorships in 13 railroad companies, namely:

American Sugar Refining Co............
..1

Baldwin Locomotive Works............
1

Colorado Fuel & Iron Co............
1

Inter-Continental Rubber Co............
1

International Agricultural Corporation............
1

International Harvester Co............
..1

International Paper Co............
.1

Lackawanna Steel Co............
..2

National Biscuit Co............
..1

Pullman Co............
..1

United States Rubber Co............
..1

United States Steel Corporation............
..2

Virginia-Carolina Chemical Co............
.1

Westinghouse Electric & Manufacturing Co............
.2

having total capitalization of $2,745,000m000 and total gross earn-
ings in excess of $1,024,000,000.

Ten directorships in 8 utility companies, namely:

American Light & Traction Co............
.1

American Telephone & Telegraph Co............
..2

Chicago Elevated Railways............
..1

Commonwealth Edison Co............
1

Consolidated Gas Co............
.2

Interboro Metropolitan Co. and Interboro Rapid Transit
Co............
1

New York Railways Co............
.1

Philadelphia Co............
..1

having total capitalization of $1,655,000,000 and total gross earnings
in excess of $317,000,000.

In all, 149 directorships in 82 companies with total assets or capitalization of $18,165,000,000.

In addition, the National Bank of Commerce has two voting trustees
each in the voting trusts of the stock of the Guaranty Trust Co. and
Southern, and one voting trustee each in the voting trusts of the stock
of the Bankers Trust Co., Chicago Great Western, and Interborough
Metropolitan Co., and two voting trustees in the Intercontinental
Rubber Co., and had one voting trustee in the expired voting trust of
the stock of the Northern Pacific Railway.

HANOVER NATIONAL BANK

The Hanover National Bank has 14 directors in 9 banks and trust companies, namely:

Bankers Trust Co............
..1
Central Trust Co............
1
Chemical National Bank............
1
Equitable Trust Co............
1
First National Bank............
..1
National City Bank............
1
New York Trust Co............
..2
Union Trust Co............
.4
United States Trust Co............
.2

having total resources of $1,102,000,000 and total deposits of $794,000,000.

Two directorships in two insurance companies, namely:

Continental Insurance Co............
1
Fidelity & Casualty Co............
1

having total assets of $37,000,000.

Thirteen directorships in 11 railroad systems, namely:

Chicago, Milwaukee & St. Paul............

1

Chicago, Rock Island & Pacific Railway. And Rock Island Co............

1

Delaware, Lackawanna & Western............

..1

Missouri, Kansas & Texas............

1

Missouri Pacific............

1

New York Central & Hudson River............

.1

New York, New Haven & Hartford............

.1

Northern Pacific............

1

St. Louis & San Francisco............

1

Southern Pacific............

2

Union Pacific............

2

having total capitalization of $5,555,000,000 and a total mileage of 75,400.

One directorship in one express company, namely, Wells-Fargo & Co., having a total capitalization of $24,000,000 and total gross annual earnings of $25,000,000.

Four directorships in three producing and trading companies, namely:

Chicago, Burlington & Quincy............

2

Delaware, Lackawanna & Western............

.2

Great Northern............

1

Louisville & Nashville............

.1

New York, New Haven & Hartford............

1

Reading Co............

..1

Southern............

..1

Chicago, Rock Island & Pacific Railway. And Rock Island Co............

..1

Erie...

..1

Lehigh Valley............

..1

New York Central & Hudson River............

1

Northern Pacific............

..3

Seaboard Air Line............

1

having a total capitalization of $4,839,000,000, and a total mileage of 66,400.

One directorship in 1 express company, namely, Adams Express Co., having a total capitalization of $48,000,000 and gross annual earnings of $33,000,000.

One directorship in 1 steamship company, namely, International Mercantile Marine, having a total capitalization of $173,000,000 and gross annual earnings of $39,000,000.

Thirteen directorships in 13 producing and trading companies, namely:

American Agricultural Chemical Co............
1

American Car & Foundry Co............
..1

American Smelting & Refining Co............
..1

International Harvester Co............
..1

National Biscuit Co............
.1

United States Rubber Co............
.1

Westinghouse Electric & Manufacturing Co............
1

American Can Co............
.1

American Locomotive Co............
.1

International Agricultural Corporation............
.1

International Paper Co............
.1

Pullman Co............
1

United States Steel Corporation............
.1

having a total capitalization of $2,471,000,000 and gross annual earnings of $950,000,000.

Six directorships in five public utility companies, namely:

American Can Co............
.3

American Locomotive Works............
..1

Baldwin Locomotive Works............
1

International Agricultural Corporation............
4

International Harvester Co............
2

International Nickel Co............
2

International Paper Co............
..2

National Biscuit Co............
..1

Pullman Co............
1

United States Rubber Co............
.1

United States Steel Corporation............
..4

Westinghouse Electric & Manufacturing Co............
..2

having a total capitalization of $2,294,000,000 and total gross income in excess of $979,000,000.

Seven Directorships in 5 public utility companies, namely:

American Light & Traction Co............
.1
American Telephone & Telegraph Co............
..3
Consolidated Gas Co............
.1
Hudson Companies & Hudson & Manhattan R.R............
.1
Philadelphia Co............
..1

having a total capitalization of $1,124,000,000 and total gross income in excess of $254,000,000.

In all, a total of 144 directors in 63 companies with total assets or capitalization of $14,416,000,000.

In addition the Astor Trust Co. has 1 voting trustee each in the voting trusts of the stock of International Agricultural Corporation, International Nickel Co., and Southern, 2 voting trustees in the Intercontinental Rubber Co., and 3 voting trustees each of the Bankers and Guaranty Trust Companies.

NEW YORK TRUST CO.

The New York Trust Co. of New York have 21 directorships in 12 banks and trusts companies, namely:
Continental & Commercial National Bank of Chicago............
1
First National Bank of Chicago............
1
Merchants Loan & Trust Co., Chicago............
.2
Astor Trust Co., New York............
.1

First National Bank, New York............
3
American Telephone & Telegraph Co............
.2
Consolidated Gas Co............
1
Hudson Co. & Hudson & Manhattan RR Co............
1
International Traction Co. of Buffalo............
1
Philadelphia Co............
.1

having a total capitalization of $1,116,000,000 and total gross annual earnings of $260,000,000.

In all, 67 directors in 48 corporations with total assets or capitalization of $11,527,000,000.

Also, the Chase International Bank has one voting trustee each in the voting trusts of the stock of the Chicago Great Western, Southern, and Guaranty Trust Co.

ASTOR TRUST CO.

Astor Trust Co. has 64 directorships in 17 banks and trust companies, namely:
Continental & Commercial National Bank, Chicago............
1
Continental & Commercial Trust & Savings Bank, Chicago............
1
Merchants Loan & Trust Co., Chicago............
1
American Exchange National Bank, New York............
2

Bank of Manhattan Co., New York............
.1
Bankers Trust Co., New York............
.14
Chase National Bank, New York............
.3
Chemical National Bank, New York............
4
Farmers Loan & Trust Co., New York............
.3
First National Bank, New York............
4
Guaranty Trust Co., New York............
11
Liberty National Bank, New York............
8
Mechanics & Metals National Bank, New York............
..2
National Bank of Commerce, New York............
..6
New York Trust Co., New York............
..1
Union Trust Co., New York............
.1
United States Trust Co., New York............
..1

total resources of $1,857,000,000 and total gross deposits $1,370,000,000.

Seventeen directorships in 9 insurance companies, namely:
American Surety Co............
.4

Continental Insurance Co............
..2
Equitable Life Assurance Society............
..2
Fidelity & Casualty Co............
..1
German-American Insurance Co............
1
Home Insurance Co............
..2
Mutual Life Insurance Co............
.3
New York Life Insurance Co............
.1
Northwestern Mutual Life Insurance Co............
1

having total assets of $2,166,000,000.
Thirty directorships in 18 railroad systems, namely:
Chicago, Burlington & Quincy............
.1
Chicago, Rock Island & Pacific Railway. Rock Island Co............
3
Delaware & Hudson Co............
2
Delaware, Lackawanna & Western............
1
Denver & Rio Grande............
.1
Erie
.3

Illinois Central............
2
Lehigh Valley............
.2
Missouri Pacific............
.1
New York Central & Hudson River............
..1
New York, New Haven & Hartford............
..2
Northern Pacific............
.2
Pere Marquette............
..1
Reading Co............
1
Seaboard Air Line............
.2
Southern Pacific............
.2
Southern............
.1
Union Pacific............
..2

having a total capitalization of $6,903,000,000 and a total mileage of 88,200.

Two directorships in 2 express companies, namely:
Adams Express Co............
1
Wells, Fargo & Co............
1

Total Capitalization of $72,000,000 and total gross income of $58,000,000.

Twenty-four directorships in 12 producing and trading companies, namely:

National City Bank, New York............
.3

United States Trust Co., New York............
..3

Continental & Commercial Trust & Savings Bank of Chicago ....
.1

First Trust & Savings Bank of Chicago............
.1

Illinois Trust & Savings Bank of Chicago............
.2

Farmers Loan & Trust Co. of New York............
..1

Hanover National Bank, New York............
..2

having total resources of $1,414,000,000 and total gross deposits of $1,069,000,000.

Six directorships in 6 insurance companies, namely:

Equitable Life Assurance Society............
.1

German-American Insurance Co............
..1

Home Insurance Co............
..1

Metropolitan Life Insurance Co............
1

Mutual Life Insurance Co............

.1

New York Life Insurance Co............

1

having total assets of $2,184,000,000.

Twenty-three directorships in 14 railroad systems, namely:

Baltimore & Ohio............

.2

Chicago, Milwaukee & St. Paul............

1

Chicago, Rock Island & Pacific Railway. And Rock Island Co............

.2

Erie

3

New York Central & Hudson River............

..1

Pere Marquette............

..2

Southern............

2

Chicago, Burlington & Quincy............

..1

Chicago & North Western............

.2

Delaware, Lackawanna & Western............

1

Louisville & Nashville............

1

Northern Pacific............

.1

Seaboard Airline............
.3
Wabash......
..1

having a total capitalization of $5,244,000,000 and a total mileage of 81,400.

One directorship in 1 steamship company, namely, International Mer

One directorship in 1 producing and trading company, namely, Lackawanna Steel Co., having total capitalization of $77,000,000 and total income of $21,000,000.

In all, 10 directorships in 10 corporations having total capitalization or assets of $2,443,000,000.

CONTINENTAL & COMMERCIAL NATIONAL BANK OF CHICAGO, ILL.

The Continental & Commercial National Bank of Chicago, Ill., have 24 directorships in 6 banks and trust companies, namely:

New York Trust Co., New York............
1
National City Bank, New York............
1
Astor Trust Co., New York............
1
Merchants Loan & Trust Co., Chicago............
1
Continental & Commercial Trust & Savings Bank, Chicago............
.17
Central Trust Co., Chicago............
3

having total resources of $506,000,000, and gross deposits of $343,000,000.

Two directorships in 2 insurance companies, namely:

Equitable Life Assurance Society............

.1

Home Insurance Co............

..1

having total assets of $530,000,000.

Eleven directorships in 9 railroad systems, namely:

Atchison, Topeka & Santa Fe............

.1

Chicago, Burlington & Quincy............

1

Chicago Great Western............

1

Chicago, Milwaukee & St. Paul............

3

Erie...

....................1

Great Northern............

..1

Illinois Central............

1

Southern.........

1

Union Pacific............

..1

having a total capitalization of $3,721,000,000 and total mileage of approximately 59,000.

Nine directorships in 7 producing and trading companies, namely:

Mercantile Marine, having a total capitalization of $173,000,000 and gross annual income of $39,000,000.

Fifteen directorships in 7 producing and trading companies, namely:

International Harvester Co............
..3

International Paper Co............
.1

Lackawanna Steel Co............
2

National Biscuit Co............
..1

Pullman Co............
..3

Standard Oil Co. of new Jersey............
.2

United States Steel Corporation............
3

having a total capitalization of $2,006,000,000 and a gross annual income in excess of $852,000,000.

Eight directorships in 7 public utility companies, namely:

American Telephone & Telegraph Co............
.1

Commonwealth Edison Co............
..1

Consolidated Gas Co............
1

Hudson Cos. & Hudson & Manhattan R.R............
..2

Philadelphia Co............
.1

Philadelphia Rapid Transit Co...........

..1

United Railways. Investment Co...........

1

having a total capitalization of $1,387,000,000 and gross annual earnings of $299,000,000.

In all, 74 directorships in 47 corporations with total capitalization and resources of $12,408,000,000.

Also the New York Trust Co. had 1 voting trustee each in the expired trust for stock of the International Harvester Co. and St. Louis & San Francisco.

BLAIR & CO., OF NEW YORK

Blair & Co., of New York, have 8 directorships in 7 banks and trust companies, namely:

Astor Trust Co., New York...........

..1

Bankers Trust Co., New York...........

..1

First National Bank, New York...........

.1

Guaranty Trust Co., New York...........

.1

Mechanics & Metals National Bank, New York...........

1

National Bank of Commerce, New York...........

1

New York Trust Co., New York...........

..2

having total resources of $953,000,000 and total deposits of $665,000,000.

Three directorships in 3 railroad companies, namely:

Denver & Rio Grande............

..1

Missouri Pacific............

1

Seaboard Air Line ....

1

having total capitalization of $754,000,000 and total mileage of 12,000.

One directorship in 1 producing and trading company, namely, Lackawanna Steel Co., having total capitalization of $77,000,000 and total gross annual income of $21,000,000.

In all, 12 directorships in 11 corporations having capitalization or resources of $1,784,000,000.

Blair & Co. also had 1 voting trustee in the expired voting trust of the St. Louis & San Francisco Railroad.

SPEYER & CO., OF NEW YORK

Speyer & Co., of New York, have 1 directorship in each of 4 banks and trust companies, namely:

Girard Trust Co., Philadelphia............

.1

Bank of Manhattan Co., of New York............

.1

Central Trust Co., New York............

..1

Union Trust Co., New York............

.1

having total capitalization of $309,000,000 and total deposits of $237,000,000.

One directorship in each of 5 railroad companies, namely:

Baltimore & Ohio............
1

Chicago, Rock Island & Pacific Railway. And Rock Island Co............
..1

Missouri, Kansas, & Texas............
..1

Missouri Pacific............
1

St. Louis & San Francisco............
1

having total capitalization of $2,057,000,000 and total mileage of 30,000.

American Sugar Refining Co............
1

Armour & Co............
3

Baldwin Locomotive Works............
.1

Intercontinental Rubber Co............
..1

International Harvester Co............
1

Pullman Co............
1

United States Steel Corporation............
.1

having total capitalization of $1,944,000,000 and a gross annual income in excess of $792,000,000.

Three directorships in 3 public utility companies, namely:

Chicago Elevated Railways............

1

Commonwealth Edison Co., Chicago............

1

Hudson COs and Hudson & Manhattan R.R............

..1

having a total capitalization of $268,000,000 and a total income of $26,000,000.

In all, 49 directorships in 27 corporations with capitalization or resources of $6,969,000,000.

FIRST NATIONAL BANK OF CHICAGO

The First National Bank of Chicago have 29 directorships in 6 bank and trust companies, namely:

First Trust & Savings Bank, Chicago............

..24

Illinois Trust & Savings Bank, Chicago............

.1

Chase National Bank, New York............

1

Equitable Trust Co., New York............

.1

First National Bank, New York............

.1

New York Trust Co., New York............

..1

having total resources of $610,000,000 and total deposits of $457,000,000.

Two directorships in 1 insurance company, namely, Equitable Life Assurance Society, having total assets of $504,000,000.

Fifteen directorships in 14 railroad systems, namely:

Baltimore & Ohio............

.1

Chicago, Burlington & Quincy............

.2

Chicago Great Western............

.1

Chicago & North Western............

.1

having total resources of $199,000,000 and total deposits of $165,000,000.

One directorship in 1 producing and trading company, namely, United States Steel Corporation, having a total capitalization of 1,440,000,000 and total gross annual earnings of $615,000,000.

Four directorships in 3 public utility companies, namely:

American Telephone & Telegraph Co............

.1

Boston Elevated Railway............

.2

Massachusetts Gas COs............

1

having a total capitalization of $756,000,000 and total gross annual earnings of $207,000,000.

In all, 8 directorships in 6 corporations having total resources or capitalization of $2,395,000,000.

LEE HIGGINSON & CO.

Lee Higginson & Co., of Boston, have 1 directorship in each of 3 banks and trust companies, namely:

First National............

.1

National Shawmut............

.1

Old Colony Trust of Boston............

.1

having total resources of $293,000,000 and total deposits of $237,000,000.

One directorship in 1 railroad system, Louisville & Nashville, having a capitalization of $196,000,000 and a total mileage of 5,000.

One directorship in each of 4 producing and trading companies, namely:

American Agricultural Chemical............

..1

General Electric............

1

United Fruit............

..1

United States Steel............

1

having a total capitalization of $1,655,000,000 and total gross annual earnings in excess of $688,000,000.

One directorship in each of 3 public utility corporations, namely:

American Telephone & Telegraph............

1

Interborough Metropolitan (and Interborough Rapid Transit Co.)
....
..1
Massachusetts Electric COs............
..1
Denver & Rio Grande............
..1
Erie...
1
Great Northern............
.1
Missouri Pacific............
.1
New York Central & Hudson River............
.1
Pere Marquette............
.1
Seaboard Air Line............
.1
Southern Pacific............
1
Union Pacific............
.1
Wabash......
..1

having a total capitalization of $5,866,000,000 and total mileage of 78,000.

Nine directorships in 7 producing companies, namely:

Colorado Fuel & Iron Co............
..1

General Electric Co............
1
International Harvester Co............
.3
Lackawanna Steel Co............
.1
National Biscuit Co............
1
Pullman Co............
.1
United States Steel Co............
1

having a total capitalization of $2,041,000,000 and a total income of $926,000,000.

In all, 55 directorships in 28 companies, having a capitalization of $9,021,000,000.

ILLINOIS TRUST AND SAVINGS BANK, CHICAGO

The Illinois Trust and Savings Bank, Chicago, has 12 directorships in 9 banks and trust companies, namely:

First National Bank, Chicago............
.1
First Trust & Savings Bank, Chicago............
.1
Merchants Loan & Trust, Chicago............
.2
Bankers Trust, New York............
..1
Chase National, New York............
.1

First National, New York............

2

National Bank of Commerce, New York............

1

New York Trust............

.2

United States Trust............

.1

having total resources of $1,075,000,000 and total deposits of $778,000,000.

One directorship in 1 insurance company, namely, Mutual Life, of New York, having total assets of $587,000,000.

One director in each of 5 railroad systems, namely:

Chicago, Burlington & Quincy............

.1

Chicago & Northwestern............

..1

Chicago, Rock Island & Pacific............

1

Great Northern............

.1

Illinois Central............

..1

having a total capitalization of $1,779,000,000 and total mileage of 37,000.

Four directorships in 3 producing and trading companies, namely:

Baldwin Locomotive Works............

.1

Lackawanna Steel............

.1

Pullman Co............
2

having a total capitalization of $251,000,000 and total gross annual earnings of $90,000,000.

Six directorships in 4 public utility corporations, namely:

American Telephone & Telegraph............
1

Chicago Elevated Railways............
..1

Chicago Railways Co............
1

Commonwealth Edison, Chicago............
.3

having a total capitalization of $907,000,000 and total gross annual earnings of $217,000,000.

In all, 28 directorships in 22 companies having total resources or capitalization of $4,599,000,000.

KIDDER, PEABODY CO.

Kidder, Peabody & Co., of Boston and New York, have 3 directorships in 2 banks and trust companies, namely:

Old Colony Trust Co............
1

National Shawmut Bank............
..2

having a total capitalization of $1,055,000,000, and total gross annual earnings of $221,000,000.

In all, 11 directorships in corporations having total resources or capitalization of $3,199,000,000.

J.P. MORGAN & CO. AND ASSOCIATES

J.P. Morgan and Co. and the Guaranty Trust Co. have three firm members or directors in common, Henry P. Davison, William H. Porter, and Thomas W. Lamont , and the two first named, together with George F. Baker, a director of the First National Bank, are voting trustees of the stock of such trust company.

J.P. Morgan & Co. and the Bankers Trust Co. have three firm members or directors in common, Henry P. Davison, William H. Porter, and Thomas W. Lamont, and the first named and Daniel G. Reid are two of the three voting trustees of the stock of such trust company; George W. Perkins having also been one of such voting trustees until he retired from the firm of J.P. Morgan & Co.

J.P. Morgan & Co. and the First National Bank have three firm members or directors in common, namely, J.P. Morgan, Henry P. Davison, and Thomas W. Lamont.

The First National Bank and the Guaranty Trust Co. have three directors in common, namely, George F. Baker, Henry P. Davison, are voting trustees of the stock of such trust company.

The First National Bank and the Bankers Trust Co. have five directors in common, namely: Henry P. Davison, A.B. Hepburn, F.L. Hine, Thomas W. Lamont, and C.D. Norton, and the first named is a voting trustee of the stock of such trust company.

The Guaranty Trust Co. and the Bankers Trust Co. have nine directors in common, namely, E.C. Converse, T. de W. Cuyler, H.P. Davison, Thomas W. Lamont, Edgar L. Marston, G.W. McGarrah, William H. Porter, Daniel G. Reid, and A.H. Wiggin; and Henry P. Davison is a voting trustee of the stock of each.

Of the nine directors of the Chase National Bank, five are also directors of the First National Bank.

Two members of J.P. Morgan & Co., 3 directors of the First National Bank, 12 directors of the Guaranty Trust Co., 4 directors of the Bankers

Trust Co., and 3 directors of the National City Bank are also directors of the National Bank of Commerce of New York.

Statement of corporations having as directors both members of J.P. Morgan & Co. and directors of First National Bank (New York)—-Continued.

Name capitalization	Resources or Directorships Held By Morgan & Co.	Directorships Held By First National Bank
Public-Utilities Corporations		
American Telephone & Telegraph Co.	621,000,000	George F. Baker
	H.P. Davison	H.P. Davison
		J.J. Mitchell
Total for all companies....		7,848,000,000

Corporations in which George F. Baker and members of J.P. Morgan & Co. are co-directors.

Resources
Bank and trust companies:

Astor Trust Co.	$27,000,000
First National Bank	149,000,000
Guaranty Trust Co.	232,000,000
National Bank of Commerce	190,000,000
Total resources of 4 banks and trust companies	$598,000,000

Assets
Insurance Companies:

Mutual Life Insurance Co.	587,000,000

Capitalization

Transport systems:

Adams Express Co.	$48,000,000
Chicago Great Western	128,000,000
Erie	418,000,000
Lehigh Valley	130,000,000
New York Central	1,150,000,000
New York, New Haven & Hartford	385,000,000
Northern Pacific	439,000,000
Reading Co.	366,000,000
Southern*	420,000,000
Total capitalization of 9 transportation systems	3,484,000,000

Producing and trading companies:

International Harvester Co.	160,000,000
Pullman Co.	120,000,000
United States Steel Corporation	1,440,000,000
Total capitalization of producing and trading corporations	1,720,000,000

*Mr. Baker is a voting trustee, but not director.

Statement of corporations having as directors both members of J.P. Morgan & Co. and directors of First National Bank (New York)—continued.

Name	Resources or capitalization	Directorships held by Morgan & Co.	Directorships held by First National Bank
New York Central &	1,150,000,000	J.P. Morgan	Geo. F. Baker J.P. Morgan

Hudson River RR			
New York, New Haven & Hartford RR	385,000,000	do	Geo. F. Baker J.P. Morgan
Norfolk & Western	217,000,000	T.W. Lamont J.P. Morgan, jr. Chas. Steele	Geo. F. Baker G.F. Baker, jr. A.C. James T.W. Lamont
Northern Pacific Railway	439,000,000	T.W. Lamont J.P. Morgan, jr. Chas. Steele	Geo. F. Baker G. F. Baker, jr. T.W. Lamont A.C. James
Reading Co.	366,000,000	E.T. Stotesbury	Geo. F. Baker
Southern Railway	420,000,000	J.P. Morgan* Chas. Steele	Geo. F. Baker G.F. Baker, jr. H.C. Fahnestock
Adams Express Co.	48,000,000	do	J.P. Morgan* Geo. F. Baker
Total of transportation systems	3,874,000,000		

Producing and Trading Corporations

Baldwin Locomotive Works	54,000,000	E.T. Stotesbury	C.D. Norton
General Electric Co.	113,000,000	Chas. Steele	J.P. Morgan J.P. Morgan
International Agricultural Corporation	34,000,000	T.W. Lamont	T.W. Lamont
International Harvester Co.	160,000,000	Geo. W. Perkins* Chas. Steele	Geo. F. Baker
Pullman Co.	120,000,000	J.P. Morgan	Geo. F. Baker J.P. Morgan J.J. Mitchell
United States Steel Corporation	1,440,000,000	do J. P. Morgan, jr. Geo. W. Perkins * Chas. Steele	Geo. F. Baker Wm. H. Moore J.P. Morgan
Westinghouse	68,000,000	T.W. Lamont	T.W. Lamont

Total producing and trading companies   1,989,000,000

Statement of corporations having as directors both members of J.P. Morgan & Co. and directors of First National Bank (New York).

Name	Resources or capitalization	Directorships held by Morgan & Co.	Directorships held by First National Bank

Banking &
Trust Companies Resources

Astor Trust Co. $27,000,000   H.P. Davison   T.W. Lamont
                                    T.W. Lamont   H.P. Davison
W. H. Porter   F.L. Hine

Chemical   40,000,000   H.P. Davison   T.W. Lamont
National Bank   Wm. H. Porter   H.P. Davison

Liberty   29,000,000   H.P. Davison   H.P. Davison
National Bank   F.L. Hine
                                                        Geo. F. Baker

National Bank   190,000,000   H.P. Davison   H.P. Davison
Of Commerce   J.P. Morgan, jr.   F.L. Hine
New York

New York Trust Co. 54,000,000   Geo. W. Perkins   Jas. A. Blair
                                    (partner of A.C. James
                                    Morgan & Co. J.J. Mitchell
                                    until recently)

Bankers' Trust Co. 205,000,000   H.P. Davison   H.P. Davison
                                    T.W. Lamont   A.B. Hepburn
                                    W.H. Porter   F.L. Hine
                                                        T.W. Lamont
                                                        C.D. Norton

Guaranty Trust Co. 232,000,000   H.P. Davison   G.F. Baker
T.W. Lamont   H.P. Davison
W. H. Porter   T.W. Lamont

Total of banks and trust companies	777,000,000		
Insurance Companies	Assets		
Mutual Life Insurance Co.	$587,000,000	Wm. H. Porter	G.F. Baker
Transportation Systems	Capitalization		
Chicago Great Western	128,000,000	J.P. Morgan* Chas. Steele	G.F. Baker* J.P. Morgan*
Erie Railroad Co.	418,000,000	W.P. Hamilton Geo. W.	Geo. F. Baker
Perkins* Chas. Steele	*		
International Mercantile Marine Co.	173,000,000	J.P. Morgan* J.P. Morgan, jr. Chas. Steele Geo. W. Perkins**	J.P. Morgan*
Lehigh Valley	130,000,000	Chas. Steele E.T. Stotesbury	Geo. F. Baker Wm. H. Moore

voting trustee, not director** until recently a partner of Morgan & Co.

Public utilities corporations:
American Telephone & Telegraph Co.   621,000,000

Total resources, assets, or capitalization of all above 7,010,000,000

Corporations in which George F. Baker and members of J.P. Morgan & Co. are co-voting trustees.

Resources

Banks and trust companies:
Guaranty Trust Co. $232,000,000

Capitalization

Transportation systems:
Chicago Great Western   128,000,000
Southern   420,000,000

Corporations in which members of J.P. Morgan & Co. and the National City Bank are co-directors

Resources

Bank and Trust companies:
Guaranty Trust Co. $232,000,000
National Bank of Commerce   190,000,000
New York Trust Co.   63,000,000
Total resources of above 3 institutions $485,000,000

Assets

Life insurance companies:
Mutual Life of New York $587,000,000

Capitalization

Transportation systems:

Atchison, Topeka & Santa Fe	$627,000,000
International Mercantile Marine Co.	173,000,000
New York Central & Hudson River	1,150,000,000
New York, New Haven & Hartford	385,000,000
Northern Pacific	439,000,000
Reading Co.	366,000,000
Total Capitalization of above 6 systems	3,140,000,000
Producing and trading corporations:	
Baldwin Locomotive Works	54,000,000
International Harvester Co.	160,000,000
United States Steel Corporation	1,440,000,000
Total capitalization of above 3 corporations	1,654,000,000
Total resources or capitalization of all above	5,866,000,000

First, through consolidation of competitive or potentially competitive banks and trust companies, which consolidation in turn have recently been brought under sympathetic management.

Second, through the same powerful interests becoming large stockholders in potentially competitive banks and trust companies. This is the simplest way of acquiring control, but since it requires the largest investment of capital, it is the least used, although recent investments in that direction for that apparent purpose amount to tens of millions of dollars in present market values.

Third, through the confederation of potentially competitive banks and trust companies by means of the system interlocking directories.

Fourth, through the influence which the more powerful banking houses, banks, and trust companies have secured in the management of insurance companies, railroads, producing and trading corporations, and public utility corporations, by means of stockholding, voting trusts, fiscal agency contracts, or representation upon their boards of directors, or through supplying the money requirements of railway, industrial,

and public utilities corporations and thereby being enabled to participate in the determination of their financial and business policies.

Fifth, through partnership or joint account arrangements between a
few of the leading banking houses, banks, and trust companies in the
purchase of security issues of the great interstate corporations, accom-
panied by understandings of recent growth—sometimes called "banking ethics"—which have had the effect of effectually destroying
competition between such banking houses, banks, and trust companies
in the struggle for business or in the purchase and sale of large issues of
such securities.

THE FINAL REPORT OF THE PUJO COMMITTE

Fifth, through partnership or joint account arrangements between a
few of the leading banking houses, banks, and trust companies in the
purchase of security issues of the great interstate corporations, accom-
panied by understandings of recent growth—sometimes called "banking ethics"—which have had the effect of effectually destroying
competition between such banking houses, banks, and trust companies
in the struggle for business or in the purchase and sale of large issues of
such securities.

SECTION 4.—AGENTS OF CONCETRATION

It is a fair deduction from the testimony that the most active agents
in forwarding and bringing about the concentration of control of
money and credit through one or another of the processes above
described have been and are-

J.P. Morgan & Co.

First National Bank of New York

National City Bank of New York

Lee, Higginson & Co., of Boston and New York

Kidder, Peabody & Co., of Boston and New York

Kuhn, Loeb & Co.

We shall describe,

First, the members of this group separately, showing the part of each in the general movement and the ramifications of its influence:

Corporations in which directors of the First National Bank and the National City Bank are co-directors

Resources

Banks and trust companies:

Farmers' Loan & Trust Co.	$135,000,000
Guaranty Trust Co.	232,000,000
Hanover National Bank	126,000,000
National Bank of Commerce	190,000,000
New York Trust Co.	63,000,000
United States Trust Co.	77,000,000

Total resources of above 6 banks and trust companies $823,000,000

Assets

Insurance companies:

Mutual Life Insurance Co.	$587,000,000

Capitalization

Transportation systems:

Delaware, Lackawanna & Western	$31,000,000
New York Central & Hudson River	1,150,000,000
New York, New Haven & Hartford	385,000,000
Northern Pacific	439,000,000

Reading Co.	366,000,000
Seaboard Air Line	164,000,000
Total capitalization of above 6 systems	$2,535,000,000

Producing and trading companies:

Baldwin Locomotive Works	54,000,000
International Harvester Co.	160,000,000
Lackawanna Steel Co.	77,000,000
United States Steel Corporation	1,440,000,000
Total capitalization of above 4 companies	1,731,000,000

Public utility company:

Consolidated Gas Co.	200,000,000
Total resources, assets or capitalization of all above	5,876,000,000

CONCENTRATION OF CONTROL OF MONEY AND CREDIT

SECTION 1.—TWO KINDS OF CONCENTRATION

It is important at the outset to distinguish between concentration of the column of money in the three central reserve cities of the national banking system-New York, Chicago, and St. Louis-and concentration of control of this volume of money and consequently of credit into fewer and fewer hands. They are very different things. An increasing proportion of the banking resources of the country might be concentrating at a given point at the same time that control of such resources at that point was spreading out in a wider circle.

Concentration of control money, and consequently of credit, more particularly in the city of New York, is the subject of this inquiry. With concentration of the volume of money at certain points, sometimes attributed, so far as it is unnatural, to the provision of the national-banking act permitting banks in the 47 other reserve cities to deposit with those in the three central reserve cities half of their reserves, we are not here directly concerned.

Whether under a different currency system the resources in our banks would be greater or less is comparatively immaterial if they continued to be controlled by a small group. We therefore regard the argument presented to us to show that the growth of concentration of the column of resources in the banks of New York City has been at a rate slightly less than in the rest of the country, if that be the fact, as not involved in our inquiry. It should be observed in this connection, however, that the concentration of control of credit is by no means confined to New York City, so that the argument is inapplicable also in this respect.

SECTION 2.—FACT OF INCREASING CONCENTRATION ADMITTED.

The resources of the banks and trust companies of the city of New York in 1911 were $5,121,245,175, which is 21.73 per cent of the total banking resources of the country as reported to the Comptroller of the Currency. This takes no account of the unknown resources of the great private banking houses whose affiliations to the New York financial institutions we are about to discuss.

That in recent years concentration of control of the baking resources and consequently of credit by the group to which we will refer has grown apace in the city of New York is defended by some witnesses and regretted by others, but acknowledged by all to be fact.

As appears from statistics compiled by accountants for the committee, in 1911, of the total resources of the banks and trust companies in New York, the 20 largest 42.97 per cent; in 1906, the 20 largest held 38.24 per cent of the total; in 1901, 34.97 per cent.

SECTION 3.—PROCESSES OF CONCENTRATION

This increased concentration of control of money and credit has been affected principally as follows:

Second, the interrelations of members of the group; and third, their combined influence in the financial and commercial life of the country as expressed in the greater banks, trust companies and insurance companies, transportation systems, producing and trading corporations, and public utility corporations.

SECTION 5.—J. P. MORGAN & CO.

Organization-J.P. Morgan & Co. of New York and Drexel & Co. of Philadelphia are one and the same firm, composed of 11 members; J.P. Morgan, E.T. Stotesbury, Charles Steele, J.P. Morgan, jr., Henry P. Davison, Arthur E. Newbold, William P. Hamilton, William H. Porter. Thomas W. Lamont, Horatio G. Lloyd, and Temple Bowdion, George W. Perkins was a member from 1902 until January 1, 1911. As a firm, it is a partner in the London banking house of J.S. Morgan & Co. and the Paris of Morgan, Hares & Co.

General character of business.-It accepts deposits and pays interest thereon and does a general banking business. It is a large lender of money on the New York Stock Exchange. More especially it lasts as a so-called issuing house for securities; that is, as purchaser or underwriter or fiscal agent, it takes from the greater corporations their issues of securities and finds a market for them either amongst other banking houses, banks and trust companies, or insurance companies, to the general public.

Resources, deposits, and profits.-Neither the resources and profits of the firm nor its sources of profit have been disclosed. Not had your committee been able to ascertain its revenues from private purchases or sales of the securities of interstate corporations, not from such of them as it controls under voting trust, exclusive fiscal agency agreements, to other arrangements or influences, not the identity of the banks, trust companies, life insurance companies, or other corporations that have participated in its security issues except where they were for joint account.

On November 1, 1912, it held deposits of $162,491,819.65, of which $81,968,421.47 was deposited 78 interstate corporations on the directorates of 32 of which it was represented. The committee is unable to state the character of its affiliations, if any, with the 46 corporations on the directorates of which it is unrepresented by one or more members of the firm, as their identity was not disclosed.

Security issues marketed.-During the years 1902 to 1912, inclusive the firm directly procured the public marketing of security issues of corporations amounting in round numbers to $1,950,000,000, including Co. already controlled. At the same time the new holders, and upon their invitation the other stockholders also, by an agreement dated January 3, 1910, vested their shares in three trustees, Mr. Davison, Mr. Porter, and George F. Baker, president of the First National Bank, with authority to vote them for all corporate purposes and especially in the selection of the board of directors and in favor of acquiring other companies.

Through this voting trust, therefore, Morgan & Co. controls absolutely the Guaranty Trust Co. Of its capital stock of $10,000,000 the firm and individual members own $844,600 par value, Mr. Davison, Mr. Porter, and Mr. Lamont, members of the firm, are directors of the trust company. On January 2, 1912, the firm had on deposit with it $1,101,000.

Since the acquisition by Morgan & Co. of control of this trust company the latter has absorbed three others-the Morton Trust Co., the Fifth Avenue Trust Co., and the Standard Trust Co. Its resources are $232,000,000 and its deposits $189,000,000.

The Guaranty and Bankers trust Cos., thus controlled by Morgan & Co. through voting trusts, are, respectively, in point of resources and deposits, the first and second largest trust companies in the United States; nor is the former outranked in the amount of deposits by any bank of the country, and the latter by one only. Their combined resources are $437,000,000; their combined deposits, $357,000,000.

Affiliations with Astor Trust Co.—Mr. Davison, Mr. Lamont, and Mr. Porter are directors of this trust company. Including them, it also has 14 directors in common with the Bankers Trust Co. and 11 in common with the Guaranty. Its executive committee, of which Mr. Davison is chairman, is composed entirely of directors of the former. Its resources are $27,000,000; deposits, $23,000,000.

Affiliations with National Bank of Commerce.-Including the holdings of individual members of that firm, Morgan & Co. own $1,686,900 par value of the $25,000,000 of capital stock of the National Bank of Commerce, and Mr. Davison and J.P. Morgan, jr., are directors thereof. Moreover, including the former, 12 directors of the Guaranty Trust Co., which is controlled by Morgan & Co., are directors of this bank. On January 1, 1912, it held deposits of Morgan & Co. to the amount of $1,084,000/ Its resources are $190,000,000; deposits, $102,000,000.

Affiliations with Liberty National Bank. -Mr. Davison is a director and chairman of the executive committee of this bank. Including him, it also has seven directors in common with the Bankers Trust Co. and five in common with the Guaranty; and a majority of its executive committee is only issues of interstate corporations. The volume of securities privately issued or marketed by it, and of intrastate corporations, does not appear. Nor is there information available of the extent to which they participated as underwriters in issues made by banks or banking houses other than those shown on the charts and lists in evidence.

Affiliations with Bankers Trust Co.,—The Bankers Trust Co was organized in 1903. As part of the plan of organization the entire capital stock, except qualifying shares held by directors, was vested for five years by an agreement dated March 18, 1903, in three trustees, George W. Perkins, then a member of Morgan & Co., Henry P. Davison, then Vise President of the First National Bank of New York and since January

1, 1909, a member of Morgan & Co., and Daniel G. Reid, then Vice President of the Liberty National Bank and a director of United States Steel Corporation and of other affiliated corporations, who were authorized to vote the same for all corporate purposes and especially for the election of directors and in favor of the acquisition of other trust companies. On March 18, 1908, the agreement was renewed for a further period of five years. Before the expiration of that extension a new agreement was made, dated March 9, 1912, substituting George B. Case, of counsel for the company, as voting trustee in place of George W. Perkins, who had retired from the firm of Morgan & Co. Apparently Mr. Case was proposed by Mr. Davison, whose personal counsel he is.

Mr. Davison's explanation that the voting trust was devised by the "young men" who organized the company, to protect them from being despoiled of the property by promoters then at large in Wall Street, does not seem adequate when it is considered that the first board of directors of the company comprised-

Stephen Baker, then about 40 years of age and president of the Bank of Manhattan Co., on of the largest banks.

Samuel G. Bayne, now in the neighborhood of 70, then president of the Seaboard National Bank, another of the great banks.

E.C. Converse, 61 or 62 years of age, a member of the executive committee of the United States Steel Co., and then president of the Liberty National Bank.

Mr. Davison himself.

James H. Eccles, then president of the Commercial National Bank of Chicago, a former Comptroller of the Currency, and a banker of great experience.

A. Bartion Hepburn, about 45, and then vice president of the Chase National Bank, and of wide reputation and banking experience.

William Logan, of the Hanover National Bank.

Gates W. McGarrah, then president of Leather Manufacturers' National Bank, and an important man in banking circles.

George W. Perkins, then a partner of Morgan & Co.

William H. Porter, then president of Chemical National Bank.

Daniel G. Reid, then, among other things, vice president of Liberty National Bank, a director of the United States Steel Corporation, and widely known in the financial world.

Albert H. Wiggin, then vice president of the National Park Bank.

Edward C.F. Young, since deceased, president of the First National Bank of Jersey City, then over 60.

Samuel Wollverton, then president of the Gallatin National Bank; and Robert Winsor, the leading partner in Kidder, Peabody & Co., one of the great international banking houses.

Through the above-mentioned voting trust Morgan & Co. have the selection of the entire board of directors of the Bankers Trust Co. The firm and the individual members own $946,400 par value of its stock, and Mr. Davison, Thomas W. Lamont, and William H. Porter, members of the firm, are directors of the trust company. On January 2, 1912, the firm had on deposit with it $1,000,000.

The capital stock of the Bankers Trust Co. at the present time is $10,000,000; surplus, $10,000,000; undivided profits, $5,084,000; resources, $205,000,000; deposits, $168,000,000. It started, March 30, 1903, with a capital of $1,000,000 and a surplus of $500,000; and about six months later its deposits were $4,748,000.

In August, 1911, it absorbed the Mercantile Trust Co., one of the oldest and largest in New York, at that time controlled by the Equitable Life Assurance Society, a majority of whose stock was then, as now, owned by J.P. Morgan. In March, 1912, it absorbed the Manhattan Trust Co.

Its unparalleled growth, whilst long established and efficiently managed and once powerful companies such as the mercantile and Manhattan were declining until they were finally absorbed by this young rival, strikingly illustrates the power of Morgan & Co. and their allies.

Affiliations with Guaranty Trust Co.-In 1910 Henry P. Davison and William H. Porter, members of Morgan & co., in association with others, purchased from the Mutual Life Insurance Co. and Mrs. Harriman 12,000 shares—6,000 from each—of the capital stock of the Guaranty Trust Co., out of a total of 20,000. Their purpose-subsequently abandoned-was to merge this company into the Bankers, which Morgan & composed of directors and the attorney of the former. Its resources are $29,000,000; deposits, $22,000,000.

Affiliations with Chemical National Bank.-Mr. Davison and Mr. Porter are directors of this bank, the latter having been its president until he resigned in order to join the Morgan Firm. Including them, four of its eight directors are directors of the Guaranty Trust Co. On January 2, 1912, Morgan & Co. had on deposit with it $837,000. Its resources are $40,000,000; deposits, $25,000,000.

Affiliations with Equitable Life Assurance Society.-J.P. Morgan now owns and has owned since 1910 a majority of the capital stock of this great company, the resources of which are $504,000,000.

Summary of Affiliations with financial corporations.-Morgan & Co. and the nominees thus control or have a powerful voice in banks and trust companies in the City of New York with resources of $723,000,000. Its own resources are unknown, but adding only its deposits, $162,000,000, the amount becomes $885,000,000; adding the resources of Equitable Life, it becomes $1,389,000,000.

RECOMMENDATIONS AND CONCLUSIONS

SECTION 1.—EVOLUTION OF THE CONTROLLING GROUPS.

Your committee is satisfied from the proofs submitted, even in the absence of data from the banks, that there is an established and well-defined identity and community of interest between a few leaders of finance, created and held together through stock ownership, interlocking directorates, partnership and joint account transactions, and other forms of domination over banks, trust companies, railroads, and public-service and industrial corporations, which has resulted in great and rapidly growing concentration of the control of money and credit in the hands of these few men.

The bulk of the oral and documentary evidence taken before your committee was directed toward ascertaining whether, in current phrase, there is a "money trust."

If by such a trust is meant a combination or arrangement created and existing pursuant to a definite agreement between designates persons with the avowed and accomplished object of concentrating unto themselves the control of money and credit, we are unable to say that the existence of a money trust has been established in that broad bald sense of the term,

First. The first, which for convenience of statement we will call the inner group, consists of J.P. Morgan & Co., the recognized leaders, and George F. Baker and James Stillman in their individual capacities and in their joint administration and control of the First National Bank, the National Bank of commerce, the Chase National Bank, the Guaranty Trust Co., and the Bankers Trust Co., with total known resources, in these corporations alone, in excess of $1,300,000,000, and of a number of smaller but important financial institutions. This takes no account of the personal fortunes of these gentlemen.

Second. Closely allied with this inner or primary group, and indeed related to them practically as partners in many of their larger financial enterprises, are the powerful international banking houses of Lee, Higginson & Co. and Kidder, Peabody & Co., with three affiliated banks in Boston-the National Shawmut Bank, the First National Bank, and the Old Colony Trust Co.-having at least more than half of the total resources of all the Boston banks; also with interests and representation in other important New England financial institutions.

Third. In New York City the international banking house of Messrs. Kuhn, Loeb & Co., with its large foreign clientele and connections, whilst only qualifiedly allied with the inner group, and only in isolated transactions, yet through its close relations with the National City Bank and the National Bank of Commerce and other financial institutions with which it has recently allied itself has many interests in common, conducting large joint-account transactions with them, especially in recent years, and having what virtually amounts to an understanding not to compete, which is defended as a principle of "banking ethics." Together they have with a few exceptions preempted the banking business of the important railways of the country.

Fourth, In Chicago this inner group associates with and makes issues of securities in joint account or through underwriting participation's primarily with the First National Bank and the Illinois Trust & savings Bank, and has more or less friendly business relations with the Continental & Commercial National Bank, which participates at times in the underwriting of security issues by the inner group. These are the three largest financial institutions in Chicago, with combined resources (including the two affiliated and controlled State institutions of the two national banks) of $561,000,000.

Radiating from these principal groups and closely affiliated with them are smaller but important banking houses, such as Kissel Kinnicut & Co., White, Weld & Co., and Harvey Fisk & Sons, who receive large and lucrative patronage from the dominating groups and are used by the latter although the committee regrets to find that even adopting that extreme definitions surprisingly many of the elements of such a combination exist.

One of the witnesses presented a statement or argument following his examination, from which it appears that he read the charts, statistics, and other testimony produced before the committee, showing among other things the total resources of various financial, railway, and industrial corporations, as intended to imply that all such resources were in the form of actual cash. It was assumed that it would be understood that the resources of railroads include their rails, station equipment, materials, and other assets as well as their cash in hand, and that the resources of industrial corporations include their plants, accounts, and other assets, and those of financial institutions their loans, discounts, and other property and investments. There is no ground for the deduction that the term "resources" as used in the exhibits was not used in the universal acceptance of the word.

It would of course be absurd to suggest that control of the bulk of the widely distributed wealth of a great nation can be corralled by any set of men. If that is what is meant by gentlemen who deny the existence of a money trust, your committee agrees with them. Such a thing would of course be impossible, and its suggestion is ridiculous. It is not, however, necessary that a group of men shall directly control the small savings in the banks nor the scattered resources of the country in order to monopolize the great financial transactions or to be able to dictate the credits that shall be extended or withheld from the more important and conspicuous business enterprises. This is substantially what has been accomplished and fairly represents the existing condition.

Under our system of issuing and distributing corporate securities the investing public does not buy directly from the corporation. The securities travel from the issuing house through middlemen to the investor. It is only the great banks or bankers with access to the mainsprings of the concentrated resources made up of other people's money in the banks, trust companies, and life insurance companies, and with control of the machinery for creating markets and distributing securities, who have had the power to underwrite or guarantee the sale of large-scale security issues. The men who through their control over the funds of our railroad and industrial companies are able to direct where such funds shall be kept, and this to create these great reservoirs of the people's money are the ones who are in position to tap those reservoirs for the ventures in which they are interested and to prevent their being tapped for purposes of which they do not approve. The latter is quite as important a factor as the former. It is a controlling consideration in its effect on competition in the railroad and industrial world.

When we consider, also, in this connection that into these reservoirs of money and credit there flow a large part of the reserves of the banks of the country, that they are also the agents and correspondents of the out-of-town banks in the loaning of their surplus funds in the only public money market of the country, and that a small group of men and their partners and associates have now further strengthened their hold upon the resources of these institutions by acquiring large stock holdings therein, by representation on their boards and through valuable patronage, we begin to realize something of the extent to which this practical and effective domination and control over many of our greatest financial, railroad, and industrial corporations has developed, largely within the past five years, and that it is fraught with peril to the welfare of the country.

If, therefore, by a "money trust" is meant—An established and well-defined identity and community of interest between a few leaders of finance which has been created and is held together through stock holdings, interlocking directorates, and other forms of domination over banks, trust companies, railroads, public-service and industrial corporations, and which has resulted in a vast and growing concentration of control of money and credit in the hands of a comparatively few men—your committee, as before stated, has no hesitation in asserting as the result of its investigation up to this time that the condition thus described exists in this country today.

Some of the endless ramifications of this power have been traced and presented and it is upon these that we have based our findings. Many others can be fully discovered and analyzed only after a close scrutiny of the internal affairs of the great national banks that will disclose the ways in which their resources are used, to whom their funds are loaned, what securities they have been buying and selling and how their vast profits have been earned. Whilst your committee has been denied access to this data, sufficient has been learned to reveal the relations of these banks and of the State banks and trust companies and the use that has been made of them in upbuilding a power over our financial system and in consequence over our railroads and greater industries that permits real competition on a large scale in the various fields of enterprise only by sufferance, if at all.

The parties to this combination or understanding or community of interest, by whatever name it may be called, may be conveniently classified, for the purpose of differentiation, into four separate groups.

Again, to take one of several similar instances, it was impossible for your committee to learn whether the prices at which Messrs. Morgan & Co. and the First National Bank have from time to time purchased the securities of the Southern Railway (the management of which they absolutely control through the voting trust referred to) represented the fair value thereof. Assuming that in this case full value was paid, your committee is of the opinion that a banking house should not occupy a position where it can determine the prices at which a corporation shall sell security issues to it. It is a trustee for the disfranchised stockholders in as broad and unqualified a sense as is a guardian for his infant ward and should be under the same disability against dealing with its cetui que trust. The same principle is applicable with respect to the trust companies with which Messrs. Morgan and Baker stand in like relation under voting trusts and which participate in their ventures as underwriters and purchasers of securities.

The suggestion that because these corporations have boards of directors composed of men of standing they are independent, seems to us disingenuous. They are the nominees of the banking house and subject to removal by it at any election. They are not accountable to the shareholders, but to Messrs. Morgan and Baker, and are not free agents, no matter how eminently respectable and distinguished they may be.

Not only does this domination of great banks and trust companies enable the inner group and their allies to control the disposition of new security issues through the control of the main outlets therefore, but it also enables them to say what and whose securities shall not be bought and of enforcing the retention in these institutions of securities issued by them of which and independent management might consider it wise to dispose. The large holdings of the Mutual and Equitable Life Insurance Cos. of the stocks of the National Bank of Commerce and of trust companies and of certain industrial companies with which Messrs. Morgan and the National City Bank are identified, such as those of the Consolidated Gas Co. and the International Mercantile Marine Co., are a few of the numerous instances of this kind. The New York Insurance Law of 1906 allowed five years for the disposition of this class of securities. This has now been extended for a further term of five years. Yet most of these securities have a ready market.

The purchase of the Equitable Life stock by Mr. Ryan and Mr. Morgan in succession furnishes an object lesson of the value that leading financiers place on the control of corporate assets not belonging to the corporation but held in trust for other people, and a fair criterion from which to judge as jobbers or distributors of securities the issuing of which they control, but which for reasons of their own they prefer not to have issued or distributed under their own names. Messrs. Lee, Higginson & Co., besides being partners with the inner group, are also frequently utilized in this service because of their facilities as distributors of securities.

Beyond these inner groups and subgroups are banks and bankers throughout the country who cooperate with them in underwriting or guaranteeing the sale of securities offered to the public who also act as distributors of such securities. It was impossible too

Beyond these inner groups and subgroups are banks and bankers thr' less they choose to purchase part of the securities, by the payment to them of a commission. There are however occasions on which this is not the case. The underwriters are then required to take the securities. Bankers and brokers are so anxious to be permitted to participate in these transactions under the lead of the inner group that as a rule they join when invited to do so, regardless of their approval of the particular business, lest by refusing they should thereafter cease to be invited.

It can hardly be expected that the banks, trust companies, and other institutions that are thus seeking participations from this inner group would be likely to engage in business of a character that would be displeasing to the latter or that would interfere with their plans or prestige. And so the protection that can be offered by the members of this inner group constitutes the safest refuge of our great industrial combinations and railroad systems against future competition. The powerful grip of these gentlemen is upon the throttle that controls the wheels of credit and upon their signal those wheel will turn or stop.

In the case of the pending New York subway financing of $170,000,000 of bonds by Messrs. Morgan & Co. and their associates, Mr. Davison estimated that there were from 100 to 125 such underwriters who were apparently glad to agree that Messrs. Morgan & Co., the First National Bank, and the National City Bank should receive 3 per cent-equal to $5,100,000-for forming this syndicate, thus relieving themselves from all liability, whilst the underwriters assumed the risk of what the bonds would realize and of being required to take their share of the unsold portion.

This transaction furnishes a fair illustration of the basis on which this inner group is able to capitalize its financial power. Included among the underwriters are the banks and trust companies that are controlled by Messrs. Morgan, Baker, and Stillman under voting trusts, through stock ownerships, and in the other ways described. Thus, they utilize this control for their own profit and that of the stockholders of the institutions. But the advantage to the depositors whose money and credit may be used in financing such enterprises is not apparent.

It may be that this recently concentrated money power so far has not been abused otherwise than in the possible exaction of excessive profits through absence of competition. Whilst no evidence of abuse has come to the attention of the committee from impartial sources, neither had there been adequate proof or opportunity for proof on the subject. Here again the data has not been available.

Sufficient has, however, been developed to demonstrate that neither potentially competing banking institutions or competing railroad or industrial corporations should be subject to a common source of private control.

Your committee is convinced that however well founded may be the assurances of good intentions by those now holding the places of power which have been thus created, the situation is fraught with too great peril to our institutions to be tolerated.

SECTION 2.—CONTROL OF MARKET FOR SECURITY ISSUES.

Through their power and domination over so many of the largest financial institutions, which, as buyers, underwriters, distributors, or investors, constitute the principal first outlets for security issues, the inner group and its allies have drawn to themselves the bulk of the business of marketing the issues of the greater railroad, producing and trading, and public-utility corporations, which, in consequence, have no open market to which to appeal; and from this position of vantage, fortified by the control exerted by them through voting trusts, representation in directorates, stock holdings, fiscal agencies, and other relations, they have been able to turn to direct the deposits and other patronage of such corporations to these same financial institutions, thereby strengthening the instruments through which they work.

No railroad system or industrial corporation for which either of the houses named has acted as banker could shift its business from one to another. Where one has made an issue of securities for a corporation the others will not bid for subsequent issues of the came corporation. Their frequent and extensive relations in the joint issue of securities has made such a modus vivendi inevitable.

This inner group and allies thus have no effective competition, either from others or amongst themselves for these large security issues, and are accordingly free to exact their own terms in most cases. Your committee has no evidence that this power is being used to oppressively and no means of ascertaining the facts so long as their profits are undisclosed.

It should be noted, however, that issues of subsidiaries of the United States Steel Corporation within the past year, amounting to $30,500,000 having been purchased by Messrs. Morgan & co., were, the greater part of them, immediately resold at a profit to Lee, Higginson & Co. and Kissel, Kinnicut & Co., when, so far as appears, the corporation could readily have saved this intermediate profit or commission by being permitted to deal directly with the banking houses which purchased the securities for distribution. It is admitted that Messrs. Morgan reaped a profit on these issues. Yet they performed no service so far as we have yet been able to learn. They neither formed the syndicate nor did they lend their names to the issue. If they wanted to market the securities we assume that it was their privilege to do so, as fiscal agents of the corporation. Otherwise, was it not their duty, situated as they were with regard to the Steel Corporation, as the supreme power therein, without whose approval no director could be named, to see to it that the best possible bargain for the corporation should be made, and not reserve to themselves a profit without risk or service? There are said to be about 130,000 shareholders in the Steel Corporation. This illustrates the vice of allowing interstate corporations to constitute exclusive fiscal agencies, which secure large revenues without performing any substantial service, and which, above all, render the corporations in question powerless to profit by competition. When we consider further that in many cases the corporation is not a free agent in thus destroying its liberty of action the practice becomes intolerable.

Mr. Morgan, however, was not one of these. He said:

Q. There is no way one man can get a monopoly of money?

A. Or control of it.

Q. He can make a try at it?

A. No, sir; he can not. He may have all the money in Christendom, but he can not do it .

Q. Let us go on. If you owned all the banks of New York, with all their resources, would you not come pretty near having a control of credit?

A. No, sir; not at all.

* * * * * * * * * * * * * * *

*** What I mean to say is this-allow me: The question of control in this country, at least is personal; that is, in money.

Q. How about credit?

A. In credit also,

Q. Personal to whom-the man who controls?

A. No, no; he never has it; he can not buy it.

Q. No; but he get-

A. All the money in Christendom and all the banks in Christendom can not control it.

Q. That is what you wanted to say, is it not?

A. Yes, sir.

And again:

Q. If you had the control of all that represents the assets in the banks of New York, you would have the control of money-of all that money?

A. No; you would not.

* * * * * * * * * * * * * * *

But money can not be controlled.

Q. Is not the credit based upon the money?

A. No, sir.

Q. It has no relation?

A. No, sir.

Q. None whatever?

A. No, sir; none whatever.

* * * * * * * * * * * * * * *

Q. Commercial credits are based upon the possession of money or property?

A. What?

Q. Commercial credits?

A. Money or property or character.

Q. Is not commercial credit based primarily upon money or property?

A. No, sir; the first thing is character.

Q. Before money or property?

A. Before money or anything else. Money can not buy it.

Q. So that a man with, character, without anything at all behind can get all the credit he wants, and a man with the property can not get it?

A. That is very often the case.

Q. But that is the rule of business?

A. That is the rule of business, sir.

* * * * * * * * * * * * * *

Q. Do you mean to say that when people lend, as when loans are made on stock-exchange collateral, to the extent of hundreds of millions of dollars, they look to anything except the collateral?

A. Yes; they do.

Q. They do?

A. Yes. Right on that point, what I did, what I used to do-and think it is pretty generally done now-is this: If I see there is a loan Mr. Smith, I say, "You call that loan right away." I would not have the loan in the box. I would not have that loan.

Q. That is not the way money is loaned on the stock exchange>

A. That is the way I loan it.

Q. No matter what collateral a man has on the stock exchange-

A. If he is not satisfactory to me, I call the loan at once, personally.

Q. I am not talking about you, personally.

A. I call that loan personally. I am not talking of anybody else's way of doing business, but I tell you what I think is the basis of business.

None of the other witnesses who were interrogated on this subject able to agree with Mr. Morgan as to the factors that enter into the c business of loaning money of collateral. Thus Mr. Baker said:

Q. As a matter of fact, Mr. Baker, in the current loans made stock-exchange collateral, does not the bank look to the security to the borrower?

A. Generally.

It is thus seen that Mr. Morgan's view that group control of credit impossible rests upon the theory that credit is not based on money resources, but wholly on character, and this even as regards loans stock exchange. This is an obvious economic fallacy, as the ev transactions of business demonstrates.

Following out this theory, Mr. Morgan further stated that he con-scious that he had the slightest power:

Q. Your power in any direction is entirely unconscious to you, not?

A. It is, sir; if that is the case.

of the reasons why they have engaged so actively in buying into banks and trust companies and in securing control thereof through voting trusts. If the controlling stock of the Equitable Life, that yields only 7 per cent on $51,000—-$3,570 per year-was worth $2,500,000 to Mr. Ryan and $3,000,000 to Mr. Morgan, why did it have that value? Was it because the life insurance company held in its treasury the majority stock of the Mercantile Trust Co., which was turned over to the Bankers Trust Co., controlled by J.P. Morgan & Co. through a voting trust, after Mr. Morgan bought Mr. Ryan's stock; and also the stocks of other banks and trust companies, including those of the National Bank of Commerce and the Fifth Avenue Trust Co? The Guaranty Trust Co., likewise controlled by Morgan & Co., through a voting trust, subsequently absorbed the Fifth Avenue Trust Co., and Messrs. Morgan, Baker, and Stillman took over one-half the holdings of the Equitable and Mutual Life Insurance Cos. of the Bank of Commerce stock.

Here, then, were stocks of five important trust companies and one of our largest national banks in New York City that had been held by these two life insurance companies. Within five years all of these stocks, so far as distributed by the insurance companies, have found their way into the hands of the men who virtually controlled or were identified with the management of the insurance companies or of their close allies and associates, to that extent thus further entrenching them.

The distinction between buying control of a bank or trust company of an industrial company or railroad is fundamental. In the latter cases the purchaser gets only the use of the assets that belong to the corporation. In the former he bargains for and gets the use of other people's money. The change of control in the latter interests only the parties to the transaction. It does not concern the public. In the former case the depositors and the public are very much interested, as must be apparent when we consider the effect of the acquisition of these bank and trust company stocks in connection with the purchases by these gentlemen of stocks in other of the great New York institutions at about that time and coincident with the establishment and renewal of voting trusts in still others.

THE PUJO REPORT (LAST SECTION)

SECTION 3.—CONCENTRATION OF CONTROL OF MONEY AND CREDIT ADMITTED.

That a rapid concentration of the sources of credit in the forms we have described has taken place in this country in very recent years was admitted by witnesses of the highest qualifications.

Q. you do not think you have any power in any department of industry in this country, do you?

A. I do not.

Q. Not in the slightest?

A. Not in the slightest.

This again illustrates that Mr. Morgan's conception of what constitutes power and control in the financial world is so peculiar as to invalidate all his conclusions based upon it.

It seems to your committee that among other things his testimony as to the circumstances under which he obtained control of the Equitable Life Assurance Co. from Mr. Ryan demonstrates his possession of power in the fullest sense, and also that he knows how to exercise it. He said:

Q.*** Did Mr. Ryan offer this stock to you?

A. I asked him to sell it to me.

Q. You asked him to sell it to you?

A. Yes.

Q. Did you tell him why you wanted it?

A. No; I told him I though it was a good thing for me to have.

Q. Did he tell you that he wanted to sell it?

A. No; but he sold it.

Q. He did not want to sell it; but when you said you wanted it, he sold it?

A. He did not say that he did not want to sell it.

Q. What did he say when you told him you would like to have it and though you ought to have it?

A. He hesitated about it, and finally sold it.

It will be noted that the only reason that Mr. Morgan gave for Mr. Ryan's surrender of the stock was that he told Mr. Ryan that he "thought it was a good thing" for him (Mr. Morgan) to have.

FIGURES 2—THRU 28 OF THE FIGURES AND ILLUSTRATIONS

FIGURE 2—MAJOR JOHN DURKEE TOWN PLANNER

Major John Durkee
TOWN PLANNER

Major John Durkee's 228-year-old plan to set aside a plot of land for public use still brings enjoyment to folks when they visit downtown Wilkes-Barre.

Durkee, who named Wilkes-Barre after John Wilkes and Col. Isaac Barre, passionate supporters of the rights of American colonists, planned the map of Wilkes-Barre.

Durkee, President of the Susquehanna Company, a group of Connecticut settlers who migrated westward, began to plan the layout for Wilkes-Barre in 1770.

The design included a diamond-shaped center for town, now known as Public Square, where many still gather for festivities, such as the famous Farmers market, which will begin its 25th season this June. A reserved site along the Susquehanna River Common, is now commonly used to jog, bike, play games, and sunbathe when the weather is warm.

Durkee's original design of Wilkes-Barre was composed of 50 small family farms, and he set aside four acres as public space and more than 30 acres near the Susquehanna River.

In 1769, Durkee, who served as a colonel in one of Connecticut's regiments during the American Revolution, led 40 Connecticut Yankees into Wilkes-Barre and built a stockade, not far from what is now Ross Street, to the dislike of Pennsylvania authorities.

Battles erupted, and now a monument commemorates Fort Durkee, the first fort built by Connecticut settlers that was used during the first Yankee-Pennomite War in 1769. The plaque can be seen as one strolls down the path along the River Common.

FIGURE 3—TIMOTHY PICKERING MEDIATOR

Timothy Pickering
MEDIATOR

Born in 1745 to a well-to-do family in Salem, Mass., Timothy Pickering graduated from Harvard University an later pursued a career in law.

An advocate of American Independence, Pickering served as quartermaster for Gen. George Washington's army.

He also made an impact in Northeastern Pennsylvania.

Pickering helped in the creation of Luzerne County, which was named for Chevalier La Luzerne, a one-time French minister to the United States.

He also was involved in the Yankee-Pennomite Wars.

In 1662, England granted Connecticut colonists land in the northern half of Pennsylvania. Yet in 1681, William Penn was given a charter which included more than two-fifths of the land sold to the Connecticut settlers.

After much bloodshed and attempted compromise, Pickering had and idea. He proposed the New Englanders be allowed to retain their land, while Pennsylvanians be compensated with public lands elsewhere. Both sides eventually accepted his suggestion.

Pickering returned to Massachusetts, where he served as secretary of state and secretary of war, serving under President Washington. Later, he was elected as a U.S. senator.

Pickering died in 1829.

FIGURE 4—ELLEN WEBSTER PALMER SOCIAL REFORMER

Ellen Webster Palmer
SOCIAL REFORMER

The inscription on a statue of Ellen Webster-

With no time for education, the boys' future didn't look promising. Palmer wanted to change that.

With community support, she started the BIA. The organization was designed to educate as well as entertain the breaker boys. Children learned reading, writing and arithmetic. Singing, debating and literacy clubs later formed.

The organization's first meetings were held in vacant stores. As the group's popularity spread, Wilkes-Barre City Council allowed it to use the fourth floor of City Hall. In 1899, the BIA constructed its own building behind City Hall, where the police station stands today.

Palmer died in 1918 at 78. The statue of her stands near the Luzerne County Courthouse.

FIGURE 5—THE RISE OF THE USE OF ANTHRACITE COAL

Jesse Fell some 189 years ago burned anthracite coal on an open grate in his tavern fireplace in Wilkes-Barre, Pennsylvania. The coal was called stone coal and this gave rise to the anthracite industry.

Until Fell's experiment the coal was only useful to blacksmiths or those who could use a forced draft. It was the open design of Fell's grate which allowed him to ignite anthracite making it suitable for household heating. This was especially important to people living in cities where wood was not readily available.

FIGURE 6—ANTHRACITE COAL PRODUCTION FROM 1820 TO 1945

YEAR	ANTHRACITE	EMPLOYEES	BITIMINOUS	IN MILLION
1820				
1869	210			
1870	7 IN 1878 COAL PRICE WAS 5.00 TON			
1870	13 MINERS PAID 12.60 WEEK			
1872	14 LABORERS PAID 9.90 WEEK			
1873	14			
1874	14 IN 1904 GOLD VALUE WAS 84 MILLION			
1875	14 SILVER WAS 53 MILLION			
1876	14 TOTAL WAS 138 MILLION			
1877	14			
1878	14 COAL VALUE WAS 550 MILLION			
1879	14			
1880	14			
1881	14 IN 1867 THERE WERE 2,904 COLLIERIES OPEN			
1882	14 IN 1868 THERE WERE 2,922 COLLIERIES OPEN			
1883	14			
1884	14			
1885	14			
1886	14			

1887	14		
1888	14		
1889	14		
1890	14		
1891	45	123000	42
1892	46		
1893	47		
1894	46		
1895	57	143605	51
1896	53	149670	50
1897	52		
1898	52		
1899	60		
1900	57	143826	80
1901	67		
1902	37		
1903	67		
1904	73	99	
1905	70	119	
1906	84	117	
1907	86	149	
1908	84	114	
1909	80	136	
1910	84	148	
1911	91	142	
1912	84	160	
1913	92	173	
1914	91	145	
1915	89	157	
1916	88	169	
1917	101	171	
1918	100	177	

1919	88	147
1920	120	167
1921	89	114
1922	54	108
1923	93	169
1924	87	128
1925	61	
1926	84	
1927	79	
1928	75	
1929	73	
1930	69	
1931	59	
1932	50	
1933	50	
1934	57	
1935	52	
1936	54	
1937	52	
1938	46	
1939	52	
1940	52	
1941	54	
1942	58	
1943	61	
1944	64	
1945	56	

FIGURE 7—BUREAU OF MINES AND THE CREATION OF THE DEPARTMENT OF MINES

Bureau of Mines

The Mines Department was established in March 3, 1870 and enacted in April 5, 1870. Prior to 1870 there were no state or federal laws governing the safety of anthracite or bituminous mining. Them mine owners considered loss of a miner to be less critical than the loss of a mule which at that time were being used to move the mine cars loaded out of the mine and to haul supplies into the mines to keep production going.

The Department of Mines was created in 1903 to overcome the deficiencies in the Bureau of Mines established in 1870. Prior to 1903 the Mines Bureau was a political arm of the mine owners and was basically a record keeping operation. Their people measured the loss of miners by accidental death in terms of tonnage of coal as if they were and expendable commodity. The 1903 Act improved the situation somewhat, but the politics up until the 1960's favored the mine owners. For all practical purposes mine production in Northeast Pennsylvania ceased to exist after 1960.

DEPARTMENT OF MINES CREATED

Act of 1903, P. L. 180, No. 137

AN ACT

To establish a Department of Mines in Pennsylvania; defining its purposes and authority; providing for the appointment of a Chief of said Department, and assistants, and fixing their salaries and expenses.

Section 1. Be it enacted, &c., That there is hereby established in Pennsylvania a Department of Mines, which shall be charged with the supervision of the execution of the mining laws of this Commonwealth, and the care and publication of the annual reports of the inspectors of coal mines and any and all other mines that may come under the provisions of the mining laws of this Commonwealth.

Section 2. The chief officer of this department shall be denominated Chief of the Department of Mines, and shall be appointed by the Governor, by and with the advice and consent of the Senate , within thirty days after the final passage of this act, and every four years thereafter, who shall be commissioned by the Governor to serve a term of four years from the date of his appointment, and until his successor is duly qualified, and shall receive an annual salary of five thousand dollars and traveling expenses; and in case of a vacancy in the office of chief of said department, by reason of death, resignation or otherwise, the Governor shall appoint a qualified person to fill such vacancy for the unexpired balance of the term.

(2 amended Jun. 7, 1915, P. L. 877, No. 390)

Section 3. The Chief of the Department of Mines shall be a competent person, having at least ten years' practical experience as a miner and the qualifications of the present mine inspectors. The said Chief of the Department of Mines, so appointed, shall, before entering upon the duties of his office, take and subscribe to the oath of office prescribed by the Constitution, the same to be filed in the office of the Secretary of the Commonwealth, and give to the Commonwealth a bond in the penal sum of ten thousand dollars, with surety, to be approved by the Governor, conditioned for the faithful discharge of the duties of his office.

Section 4. It shall be the duty of the Chief of the Department to devote the whole of his time to duties of his office, and to see that the mining laws of the State are faithfully executed; and for this purpose he is hereby invested with the same power and authority as the mine inspectors, to enter, inspect and examine any mine or colliery within the State, and the works and machinery connected therewith, and to give such aid and instruction to the mine inspectors, from time to time, as he may deem best calculated to protect the health and promote the safety of all person employed in and about the mines; and the said Chief of the Department of Mines shall have the power to suspend any mine inspector for any neglect of duty, operators setting forth that any of the mine inspectors are neglectful of the duties of their office, or are physically unable to perform the duties of their office, or are guilty of malfeasance in office, he shall at once investigate the matter; and if he shall be satisfied that the charge or charges are well founded, he shall then petition the court of common pleas or the judge in chambers, in any county within or partly within the inspection district of the said mine inspector; which court upon receipt of said petition and a report of the character of the charges and testimony produced, shall at once issue a citation, in the name of the Commonwealth, to the said inspector to appear, on not less than fifteen days' notice, on a fixed day, before said court, at which time the court shall proceed to inquire into the allegations of the petitioners, and may require the attendance of such witnesses, on the subpoena issued and served by the proper officer or officers, as the judge of the court and the Chief of said Department may deem necessary in the case; the inspector under investigation shall also have similar power and authority to compel the attendance of witnesses in his behalf. If the court shall find by said investigation that the said mine inspector is guilty of neglecting his official duties, or is physically incompetent to perform the duties of his office, or is guilty of malfeasance in office, the said court shall certify the same to the Governor, who shall declare the office vacant, and shall proceed to supply the vacancy as provided by the mining laws of the State. The cost of such investigation shall, if the charges are sustained, be imposed upon the deposed min inspector; but if charges are not sustained, the costs shall be paid out of the State Treasury, upon voucher or vouchers duly certified by said Chief of Department.

To enable said Chief of the Department of Mines to conduct more effectually his examinations and investigations of the charge and complaints which may be made by petitioners against any of the mine inspectors as herein provided, he shall have power to administer oaths and take affidavits and depositions, in form and manner provided by law: Provided, however, that nothing in this section shall be construed as to repeal section thirteen of article two of the act of Assembly, approved the second day of June, Anno Domini one thousand weight hundred and ninety-one, entitled "An act to provide for the health and safety of persons employed in and about the anthracite coal mines of

Pennsylvania, and for the protection and preservation of property connected therewith," and also articles thirteen and fourteen of an act of Assembly, approved the fifteenth day of May, Anno Domini one thousand eight hundred and ninety-three, entitled relating to bituminous coal mines, and providing for the lives, health, safety and welfare of persons employed therein."

Section 5. It shall be the duty of the Chief of the Department of Mines to take charge of, and preserve in his office, the annual reports of the mine inspectors, and transmit a synopsis of the, together with such other statistical data equipped to reproduce the same, for publication, on or before the first day of April in each year; the same to be published under the direction of the Chief of the Department of Mines. In order that the Chief of the said Department may be able to prepare, compile and transmit a synopsis of his annual report to the Governor within the time herein specified, the mine inspectors are hereby required to deliver their annual reports to the Chief of said Department on or before the twentieth day of February, in each year. In addition to the annual reports herein required of the mine inspectors, they shall furnish the Chief of the Department of Mines monthly reports, and also such special information on any subject regarding mine accidents, to other matters pertaining to mining interests, or the other safety of persons employed in and about the mines, as he at any time may require or may deem necessary, in the proper and lawful discharge of his official duties. The Chief of the Department of Mines shall also establish, as far as many be practicable, a uniform style and size of blanks for the annual, monthly and special reports of the mine inspectors, and prescribe the form and subject matter to be embraced in the text and the tabulated statements of their reports.

The Chief of the Department of Mines is hereby authorized to make such examinations and investigations as may enable him to report on the various systems of coal mining and all other mining practiced in the State, method of mining ventilation and machinery employed, the circumstances and responsibilities of mine accidents; and such other matters as may pertain to the general welfare of coal miners and others connected with mining, and the interests of mine owners and operators in the Commonwealth.

(E amended Jul. 18, 1957, P. L. 990, NP. 434)

Section 6. The Board of Examiners for the examination of applicants for mine inspectors in the Anthracite and Bituminous coal mines of the Commonwealth, the Board for the examination of applicants for mine foremen and assistant mine foremen in the anthracite mines, the Board for examination of applicants for first and second grade certificates in the Bituminous mines, and the Board styled Miners' Examining Board for applicants for certificates of competency as miners, shall send to the Chief of the Department of Mines duplicates of the manuscripts and all other papers of applicants, together with the tally-sheets and the solution of each question as given by the Examining Board, which shall be filed in the Department as public documents for a period of time not less than eight years.

(6 amended Jul. 17, 1957, P. L. 980, No. 427

Section 7. Certificates of qualification to mine foremen and assistant mine foremen in the anthracite mines shall be granted by the Chief of the Department of Mines to each applicant who has passed a successful examination. The certificates shall be in manner and form as shall be prescribed by the Chief of the Department of Mines, and a record of all certificates granted shall be kept in the department. Each certificate shall contain the full name, age, and place of birth of the applicant, and shall be to the Chief of the Department of Mines, be the State Treasury, —said fees to be put in the fund of the Department of Mines for the use of the department for inspection service. The moneys in such fund, from time to time, are hereby specifically appropriated to the Department of Mines for the purposes herein provided. In case of the loss or destruction of a certificate, the Chief of the Department of Mines shall, upon the presentation of satisfactory evidence of the loss or destruction, issue a copy of the certificate, to the original possessor, on the payment of the sum of one dollar.

(7 amended May 28, 1923, P. L. 456, No. 248)

Section 8. The Chief of the Department of Mines shall keep in the Department a journal or record of all inspections, examinations and work done under his administration, and copies of all official communications; and is hereby authorized to procure such books, instruments, and chemicals, to other tests, as may be found necessary to the proper discharge of his duties under this act, at the expense of the State. All instruments, plans, books and records pertaining to the office shall be the property of the State, and shall be delivered to his successor in office.

Section 9. (9 repealed Apr. 4, 1929, P. L. 151, No. 153)

Section 10. The Chief of the Department of Mines shall, at all times, be accountable to the Governor for the faithful discharge of his duties imposed on him by law, and the administration of his office and the rules and regulations pertaining to said Department shall be subject to the approval of the Governor.

Section 11. No person who is acting as a land agent, or as a manager, viewer or agent of any mine or colliery, shall, at the same time, serve as Chief of the Department of Mines under the provisions of this act.

Section 12. All acts or parts of acts inconsistent with this act be and the same are hereby repealed.

FIGURE 12—UNITED STATES MONETARY HIGHLIGHTS 1775 TO 1997

1775 Continental Congress authorizes paper dollars (Continentals).

1789 The Constitution empowers the Federal Government to coin money.

1792 Coinage Act of 1792 permits free coinage of gold and silver.

1806 Coinage of silver dollars suspended.

1849 Coinage of gold dollars begins.

1862- Legal Tender Acts authorize Government paper money.
1863

1863 National Bank Act ends circulation of state banknotes.

1871- Supreme Court upholds Legal Tender Acts.
1884

1873 Coinage Act of 1873 defines the dollar as a weight of gold.

1875 Specie Resumption Act authorizes redemption of greenbacks.

1879 Greenbacks return to full convertibility.

1900 Gold Standard Act places U.S. dollar on official gold standard.

1913 Federal Reserve System is created.

1933 President Roosevelt declares "bank holiday."

1933 Domestic Gold Standard is abandoned.

1933 Executive Order 6102 confiscates gold holdings.

1934 Gold Reserve Act authorizes devaluation of dollar on foreign exchange.

1935 Supreme Court upholds abrogation of gold claims on Government certificates and private contracts.

1944 Bretton Woods agreement establishes new international monetary system of fixed exchange rates.

1958-59
United States pays out 95 million ounces of gold to meet dollar claims of foreigners.

1961 International "Gold Pool" created.

1961 President Eisenhower prohibits American ownership of gold anywhere in the world.

1968 Congress removes all bullion reserve requirements for Federal Reserve Notes.

1971 President Nixon closes the "gold window."

1973 The dollar is officially devalued from $38 to $42.22 per ounce of gold.

1974 U.S. citizens permitted to hold gold in any form.

1978-80
United States sells gold reserves at public auction.

1980   Depository Institutions Deregulation and Monetary Control Act initiates financial deregulation and monetary "management."

1980   U.S. Treasury commences mintage of gold medallions.

1980   Gold Study Commission created.

1985   Gold Bullion Coin Act of 1985 authorizes mintage and issue of legal tender gold coins.

1994   U.S. Treasury authorizes redesign of U.S. Currency to foil counterfeits.

1997   Dollar Coin Act of 1997 and 50 States Commemorative Coin Program Act of 7 authorize minting of new base metal dollar and quarter coins.

FIGURE 13—MILESTONES IN THE CREATION OF AMERICAN TELEPHONE AND TELEGRAPH

1869   Elisha Gray and Enos Barton form small manufacturing firm in Cleveland, Ohio.

1872   Gray and Barton's firm re-named Western Electric Manufacturing Company.

1881   American Bell purchases controlling interest in Western Electric and makes it the manufacturer of equipment for the Bell Telephone Companies.

1899   AT&T, created in 1885, takes over AY-

1979   A Federal Communications Commission inquiry restricts AT&T from selling enhanced services except through an AT&T subsidiary, American Bell, which begins operations in 1983.

1982   AT&T and the Justice Department settle an antitrust suit that modifies the 1956 consent decree. AT&T will spin off local telephone companies and retain long-distance service, Western Electric and Bell Labs.

1984   AT&T spins off local telephone companies. Western Electric's charter is assumed by a new unit called AT&T Technologies.

1995 AT&T announces its plan for restructuring into three separate, publicly traded companies: a service company that will retain the name AT&T; a systems and technology company (Lucent Technologies) composed of Bell Labs, Network Systems, Business Communication Systems, Consumer Products and Microelectronics; and a computer company, which recently returned to the NCR name.

Lucent Technologies names Henry B. Schacht as Chairman and Chief Executive Officer, and Richard A. McGinn as President

FIGURE 14—BRINGING THE WELSH TO AMERICA

In bringing the Welsh to America from England the coal mine owners in Northeast Pennsylvania were actually doing them a favor because times were very bad in England. The English worker was being paid only one third or less of what he could earn in the mines in Northeast Pennsylvania. Therefore it was quite easy to convince the Welsh who had the coal mining experience to go to the new world. In the 1840's in England the landowners could hire men for 18 cents American a day and found this to be cheaper to dig the fields than to plow with horses. A clerk in England in 1840's earned $4.36 per week or $227 dollars per year while in the United States, even though there were hard times due to the panic of 1837 a clerk was paid $700 per year. It was very easy to convince miners in Wales to come to Northeastern Pennsylvania and earn 3 times what they could earn in Wales.

FIGURE 15—THE DORRANCETON METHODIST CHURCH

DORRANCETON

The original Dorranceton Methodist Church, Kingston, had been around since 1897 when it was dedicated on Wyoming Avenue with the first sermon delivered by Rev. C. F. Mogg of Wilkes-Barre.

According to the records at the Wyoming Historical and Geological Society, Wilkes-Barre, the original church was built at a cost of $2,000 and the lot of 100 feet by 133 feet was purchased for $1,000. The building committee consisted of J. M. Welter, A. S. Hershberger and Noah Pettebone.

The community of Dorranceton originally was part of Kingston Township, bounded by Forty-Fort, Kingston Township and Luzerne Borough and Pringle Township. It was named in honor of the Dorrance family, who were prominent.

The community consolidated with Kingston Township, now the Municipality of Kingston, in 1921. In those days, according to historical society records, there were no movies theaters, no automobiles, few telephones and a few bicycles. But, there were three churches.

The Dorranceton United Methodist Church, across Wyoming Avenue from the Nesbitt Memorial Hospital, today is a reminder of the small section of Kingston that once stood alone.

FIGURE 16—HISTORICAL MARKERS TO PAY TRIBUTE TO JUDGE JESSE FELL

On Feb, 11, exactly 189 years after his experiment which helped launch the coal industry in the Wyoming Valley, Jesse Fell will be honored for his part in history.

The ceremony will unveil a permanent historic marker on the tree lawn at the corner of East Northampton and South Washington streets, where Fell's tavern once stood.

Sponsored by the Pennsylvania Historical and Museum Commission in Harrisburg and the Wyoming Historical and Geological Society, the marker also had the support of Mayor Thomas D. McGroarty and city council. It was paid for in part by former Luzerne County District Attorney Stephen A. Teller and Kingston Councilwoman Sally Teller Lottick, who are both descendants of Fell's younger brother, Amos.

The marker is covered with cardboard until the dedication ceremony, but Teller Lottick said it reads as follows:

"Jesse Fell (1751-1830)—At his tavern here on Feb. 11, 1808, Fell burned "stone coal" successfully on an open grate. This famed experiment spurred the rise of the anthracite industry and the Wyoming Valley's growth. He was a judge, 1798-1830 and first burgess of Wilkes-Barre, 1806."

Until Fell's experiment, the coal was useful only to blacksmiths or those who could use a forced draft, Teller Lottick said. It was the open design of Fell's grate which allowed him to ignite anthracite, making it suitable for household heating. This was especially important to people living in cities, where fire wood was not readily available, she said.

Fell's hotel, built in 1787, was originally called "The Sign of the Buck," according to the Wyoming Historical and Geological Society. It was a stage coach stop on the old Easton and Wilkes-Barre Turnpike, built in 1806. It became a licensed tavern by 1823, making it the oldest licensed hotel in Wilkes-Barre.

The local historical society, one of the oldest in the United States, was founded at Old Fell House Feb. 11, 1858

The tavern was a popular meeting spot, Teller Lottick added. Town meetings were held at the site, and there are even references to it's having been used as an early courtroom.

A hotel and tavern stood on the lot until 1986, when an area hospital acquired the site and demolished the building, including the fireplace where the experiment was conducted.

The public is invited to the ceremony at 10 am on Tuesday.

FIGURE 17—THE LIFESTYLE OF THE RICH WHO HAD EXPLOITED THE RICK CAPITAL FROM COAL

For 250 years, St. Augustine was ruled first by the Spanish, briefly by the British and again by the Spanish before becoming a part of the United States in 1821. The small town was hobbled by a meager economy until 1884, when Henry Flagler arrived. An entrepreneur who had made a fortune as a founding partner of Standard Oil, Flagler saw the potential for turning St. Augustine into and American Riviera. There was plenty of sun, miles of nearby ocean beach and railway line that already extended to nearby Jacksonville. Only the luxurious accommodations were missing, and he had the money to build them.

Nothing in Florida could rival Flagler's two extravagantly elegant Mediterranean-Style hotels. At the Ponce de Leon, with its striking towers and dining room ceiling adorned in fresco, President Grover Cleveland mingled with the Vanderbuilts and Rockefellers in the winter of 1888.

FIGURE 18—WHO ARE THE RICH TODAY?

Each family keep $100,000 in after-tax income, and takes 100% of any excess. Such confiscatory taxation, wildly assuming everything else held constant, would have produced $135 billion in extra revenues in 1992. In that year, federal spending was $1,380 billion, and the deficit was $290 billion.

Nothing important to the government finance, in short, can be accomplished by making the income tax more progressive. While the largest source of government revenue, the personal income tax accounts for less than half of the federal income; payroll taxes are nearly as large, and there is also the corporate income tax and other revenues. Within the income tax progressive rates of course produce revenues, but scarcely a decisive amount in a trillion-dollar budget or six-trillion-dollar company.

This point has been made graphic by W. Kurt Hauser's famous 19.5% charts. Despite top income tax rates ranging from 28% to 91%, federal revenues have continued to hover around 19.5% of GDP. Those facing onerous rates find ways around them; in the large picture, revenue from "the rich" scarcely matters.

All of which suggests that during tax week in the House, there may be more important things to talk about. The debate over whether a $500-a-kid credit ought to phase out at $200,000 or $95,000 is, well, childish. What Congress ought to be debating is how to structure the tax system to promote economic growth. As Mr. Hauser said, "Nineteen and a half percent of a larger GDP is preferable to 19.5% of a smaller GDP." The welfare of our children will depend a lot less on any tax credit than on whether we have a healthy economy.

As it happens, the new Republican majority in the Congress has a lot of ideas about the relation between taxes and growth. The child tax credit in the House "Contract" doesn't pretend to be a growth initiative, of course, but is billed as a cash remedy to the moral problems of illegitimacy and divorce. However, the "Contract" also named specific growth initiatives including, among others, a cut in the capital gains tax. Senate Republicans are interested in measures to cut taxes on returns to savings, as a method of increasing savings, investment and growth.

And, of course, the House is gearing up for a later debate on Rep. Dick Armey's flat tax, which combines all of these ideas. It would sharply pare the top marginal rate to boost economic incentives. But it would also include a generous family allowance, not only doing what taxes can to help families, but also retaining a progressive feature in effective tax rates. It would also exempt saving return. And it's intended to drastically simplify tax returns Americans file this month.

None of these ideas has any great prospect, though, so long as tax week is about fairness and the rich. The fairness debate had been suppressed by the political and economic success of the Reagan tax cuts, which offered and indeed produced rapid economic growth by reducing high marginal tax rates that stifle incentives. "Fairness" reappeared under the aegis of former Senate Majority Leader George Mitchell in his filibuster victory over capital gains reduction in 1989, and has dominated tax debate since. Even the newly victorious Republicans have not cast off Mr. Mitchell's spell.

The Republicans are going nowhere with tax policy we predict until they take the "fairness" debate head-on and win it. Yes, if you have a tax cut it will benefit the people who pay the most taxes. But the real issue is whether it will benefit the economy, providing a bigger pie to share among the rich, the poor and the government.

FIGURE 19—COAL BREAKER BOYS
—ALL WORK, NO PLAY AND LOW PAY

Breaker boys: All work, no play and low play

During the 1800s and early 1900s, life for many little boys in the Wyoming Valley was filled with a lot of hard work.

As young as seven and eight years old, the boys would work all day long at the coal breaker. By the time they got home late at night, there was little time left for play. They would eat, sleep and get ready for the next day's work.

As they got older, most breaker boys would follow in their father's and grandfather's footsteps by becoming miners.

According to the Lackawanna County Coal Mine, in 1902, breaker boys made 13 cents per hour. Also at that time, miners made approximately $2.75 per day, laborers, 18 cents per hour, and track layers, 24 cents per hour. Children also worked in the mining industry as slate pickers, making 6 cents per hour, and when they were a little older they made 13 cents per hour as mule drivers.

FIGURE 20—FRANCIS DREXEL
—BUSINESS PARTNER OF JUNIUS AND
J. P. MORGAN WHO FOUND WAYS
TO USE THE COAL TRUST MONEY

Katherine Drexel was born in 1858 to a family of great affluence. He father, Francis Drexel, was a banking magnate and business partner of J. P. Morgan. Her uncle, Anthony Drexel, founded Drexel University. Young Katherine was a world traveler and a debutante but also was taught the importance of charity.

FIGURE 21—JOHN N. CONYNGHAM —NORTHEAST BUSINESS PARTNER OF J. P. MORGAN AND HAYFIELD HOUSE HIS MANSION

Hayfield House near Lehman now serves as the administrative offices of Penn State University's Wilkes-Barre campus. The 55-room mansion was built by John N. Conyngham II during the Depression for and estimated $1 million.

Mr. Conyngham's portrait adorns a wall in the Hayfield House living room.

A polar bear mural hangs above Mr. Conyngham's former bathtub, now in the office of Ina K. Lubin, Penn State Wilkes-Barre's director of continuing education.

FIGURE 22—CHARLES H. DOW —A PAWN OF J. P. MORGAN AND THE COAL TRUSTS

Charles H. Dow couldn't have known it, but 1896 was an auspicious time to begin his average of industrial shares. A bitter national depression, born of the panic of 1893, was near to running its course. Deflation, the curse of farmers and wage earners, seemed ready to ease its icy grip.

Only the previous year, Mr. Dow may have been among those in New York harbor who watched freighters laden with gold steaming for London. He had surely known that the gold-depleted U.S. government was days from default. But as Mr. Dow's young newspaper had chronicled, financier J. P. Morgan Sr. Had saved the day by organizing a bond syndicate. President Cleveland accepted the move reluctantly. But he had little choice: There was no Federal Reserve, and no public safety net save for the intervention of Wall Street's reigning baron.

On May 26, 1896, when the Dow Jones Industrial Average was first published, the genesis of a recovery was at hand. At the same time, a merger wave was reshaping American business. In industry after industry, giant corporations were seeking national markets-and often, monopolies.

These companies, Mr. Dow predicted, would constitute "the great speculative market" of the future. A partial list of these newly formed "trusts' included copper, glue, hay, needles, flour, sugar, lead, whiskey, plate glass, wire nails, coal and steel. Yet the trend was hardly glimpsed by many. For most Americans, business still was local: the foundry, the store, the farm. The national "economy" seemed and abstraction.

Mr. Dow's index of 12 industrials-General Electric is the lone survivor among the current 30 stocks-began at 40.94. A hostage to politics from the start, the average was buffeted by what historian Robert Sobel would call the most-important election since the Civil War. William Jennings Bryan, giving poetic voice to farmers' and Westerners' fanatical hatred of tight money, campaigned for an end to "the cross of gold." In its place, he promised silver money and inflation.

Mr. Dow, though he had been born on a Connecticut farm, thought the silver standard "folly." Indeed, anyone with a mind to invest in the shares in his newly concocted average-all of Wall Street, every banker, all the new industrialists-put in for gold and sound money. The average, which Mr. Dow figured by pencil, fell a disastrous 30% as the campaign dragged on, touching 28.48% in August.

Mr. McKinley's victory saved the gold standard, and gold strikes in the Yukon and elsewhere soon restored liquidity. Mr. Dow's average would never go so low again.

Yet when prosperity returned, it was visited on a changed country. The previous half-century had been the age of rails. Their relentless steel ribbons had been the arsenal of growth, if not exactly of democracy (fixing rates and buying legislatures being vital to the business). Railroads had become the first great national corporations. Their shares were actively traded from Boston to San Francisco; indeed, theirs and virtually none others.

On the New York Stock Exchange, 60% of the listed stocks were rails. When Mr. Dow first cobbled together an index of eleven companies in 1884, nine of those, were rails. Industrial stocks with reasonable float and liquidity were scarce.

Even National Cordage Co., a rope manufacturer and the most widely traded industrial of the Gilded Age, had, as the popular joke went, hanged itself in the panic of '93, according to James Grant's evocative biography "Bernard Baruch." General Electric itself had needed a Morgan bailout.

Stocks in general were frowned on. Share prices, often controlled, cornered or otherwise stage-managed by Wall Street pools, were subject to spectacular rises and plunges. Trading on inside information was de rigueur, and little other information existed. In 1895, when the stock exchange gingerly proposed that companies distribute an annual statement of earnings to shareholders, it was a radical step.

Prudent investors bought bonds-which is what Mr. Dow recommended to readers of the Ladies Home Journal. Stocks were the playthings of raiders and speculators. In our own age, stocks are urged on savers from toddlers on up, but one hundred years ago the notion of putting savings in industrial shares was hardly serious. It was simply too risky.

The very concept of investing-and paying up-for future profits was foreign, according to Ron Chernow, author of a forthcoming biography of John D. Rockefeller. Stocks selling for more than the issuing company's asset value were considered "watered." To gamble on them was un-Victorian speculation. Investors trusted in tangible assets and sought return from income. That is why bonds were the preferred vehicle. Among stocks, only the railroads paid dividends on a regular basis.

Yet by 1890, the railroads had covered the country and the frontier had been tamed.

FIGURE 23—ARSENE PUJO
—J. P. MORGAN ANTAGONIST AND
UNITED ATATES CONGRESSMAN

Pujo, Arsene Paulin (Dec. 16, 1861-Dec. 31, 1939), lawyer and Congressman, was born at "Rose Bluff," Calcasieu Parish, La., the third of four children of Paul and Eloise (LeBleu) Pujo. His father had emigrated from Tarbes, France to Louisiana about 1840, settling eventually in Calcasieu Parish; his mother was a native of the parish. Pujo attended public and private schools in Lake Charles, La., where his father had a store, and later read law under Judge Gabriel A. Fournet, securing admission to the bar in 1886. On Dec. 16, 1889, he married Georgia Brown of Orange, Texas, by whom he had two daughters, Elaine and Mona.

Pujo was active in the campaigns of the Anti-Lottery League of Louisiana in 1888 and 1892. In 1898 he was elected to his first public office as a delegate-at-large to the Louisiana constitutional convention, in which he served as a member of the judiciary committee. In 1902 he was elected to Congress, where he remained for five terms.

Pujo was one of eighteen Representatives and Senators named to the National Monetary Commission, established in 1908 to study banking systems throughout the world and to recommend legislation for a reorganization of the American banking system. The commission was dominated by the Republican Senate leader, Nelson W. Aldrich [q.v.] , and its report (Jan. 8, 1912) proved unsatisfactory to most Democrats and Progressives; yet it did note "an unhealthy congestion of loanable funds in great centers" and "a concentration of surplus money and available funds in New York." Pujo had in 1911 become chairman of the House Banking and Currency Committee. Receiving congressional authorization in February 1912, he headed a subcommittee (popularly known as the "Pujo Committee") which in April launched and inves-tigation of the precise extent of the "money trust." As committee counsel Pujo selected the noted New York lawyer Samuel Untermyer [q.v.], who conducted most of the spectacular hearings in which J. P. Morgan [q.v.] and other leading bankers were questioned. The committee's report, issued early in 1913, declared that there was evidence of a "well-defined...community of interest between a few leaders of finance... which has resulted in great and rapidly growing concentration of the control of money and credit" in the hands of a few men J. P. Morgan & Company being "the recognized leaders." Although most of the com-mittee's specific recommendations were ignored, the investigation helper to prepare the way for the passage of the Federal Reserve Act of 1913 and the Clayton Anti-Trust Act of 1914.

FIGURE 24—TODAYS CLASS WAR AND WHO ARE THE RICH?

In today's class war, don't shed tears for the 'slipping' rich
by Donald Kaul

Good news arrived the other day. A new survey, conducted by the U.S. Federal Reserve and the Internal Revenue Service, found that the richest Americans have stopped getting richer.

Yes, the top one-half of one percent of us-multimillionaires all-after having made out like bandits throughout the Reagan years, have paused for breath and, indeed, may even be slipping.

The study estimated that in 1989 the wealthiest half-percent controlled nearly 29 percent of U.S. private wealth. By 1992, after a recession, the figure had fallen to just under 23 percent.

That may not be reason enough to break out the party hats, but it's something.

I am not envious of rich people, any more than I am envious of a looter running down the street with a television set during a riot. In

210

both cases I am merely outraged by the injustice of the manner in which they got their booty.

Oh, not all of them, of course. There are cases in which the looter rescued the TV set from a fire, in which case he had some claim to it. And, even in rarer instances, there are deserving rich people.

But not everybody in that top half-percent is a Bill Gates or anything like him. There are people who inherited their money without ever having to lift a squash racquet to earn it. There are some (stockbrokers and lawyers, mainly) who have stolen it and avoided detection. Others are just flat overpaid.

The New York Times ran a story on executive pay a few weeks back. A well-regarded researcher in the field, Graef S. Crystal, found that only a quarter of a chief executive's pay could, on the average, be justified by either the size of his company or his performance. He found one fellow who received $15.5 million in compensation from a company that grossed only $72 million and turned in a net loss of $7.9 million.

He was at the top of the list of the overpaid, but it was a long list.

Nor do I really believe that the rich have stopped getting richer. That federal study was based on an interviews with a sampling of rich people.

They lied.

More Persuasive are some figures from a column by Marjorie Kelly, publisher of Business Ethics, a magazine.

She found that in 1992, the average chief executive officer made $2.7 million, while the average worker made $18,900. In 1993, the CEOs got raises of $600,000 while the worker got $500. In 1994, CEOs $400,000, workers $600. So, as of two years ago, the CEOs were at $3.7 million, the workers at $20,000.

American execs, then, make 187 times as much as their employees; that's compared to a 20:1 ration in Japan and 35:1 in France and Germany. (In 1970, by the way, American bosses made only 40 times more than their serfs.)

So don't tell me about class was or unleashing the power of the free enterprise system by lowering taxes on rich people. The class war has been fought. Rich people won.

I leave you with two words: Progressive taxation. It's the last weapon we poor guerrillas living in the hills have left to us. If we don't use that, we might as well be POWs.

FIGURE 25—MYTHS VERSUS REALITIES —WHO PAYS THE TAXES?

Myths Versus Realities

A number of authoritative, nonpartisan reports present a sharply different portrait of the U.S. than that which politicians of both parties are painting. Among the more dramatic disparities between political myth and reported reality:

Myth No. 1: The tax burden and who pays it. Democrats are convinced that the wealthy are getting away with murder. The GGOP has nightmares about welfare cheats, fathers on the run, and a class of idlers who live off the efforts of others.

Reality Check: The most recent data from the IRS (for 1992 returns) is explicit. More than a quarter of all federal individual income taxes is paid by the top 1% of income earners.

The IRS statistics get even more dramatic the further one slices down into the who-earns-what, who-pays-what list. Of the 112.7 million federal individual tax returns, there were 1.1 million filers who earned $181,713 or more to qualify for the top percentile. Their tax bill accounted for 27.4% of all taxes reported to the IRS that year. The top 10% of American earners paid more than half (57.5%) of all the personal income tax revenues Washington received. In all, 56.3 million filers (50% of returns) paid a staggering 94.9% of all the federal revenues collected from individuals.

Chris Edwards, an economist at the Tax Foundation think tank in Washington, notes, "On the Flip side, the 56.3 million filers representing the bottom half of income earners paid only 5.1% of all federal income taxes." This raises a question: Does it cost more than it is worth to collect taxes from this large group?

One of the paradoxes of the tax data is that while the top tax rate imposed has plunged mightily from its record of 91% in 1963 to 50% in 1982 and then to 28% in 1988, the portion of taxes actually paid by the top 1% has been rising since 1970 and has kept rising through the tax rate boosts of President Bush (to a 31% tax bite in 1991) and Clinton (to 36.9% in 1993 with a surcharge to 39% for million dollar earners).

The top 1% are not primarily heirs of the rich. IRS data indicates that 39.7% of these income earners got their money from salaries and wages, while another 22% were members of professional partnerships or ran small businesses.

FIGURE 27—NO ONE NOTICED THE 100 POINT MARK

No One Noticed 100-Point Mark

On Jan. 12, 1906, the Dow Jones Industrial Average surged above 100 for the first time.

Nobody paid any attention.

In a striking contrast to later milestones, the industrial average's first century mark-which came 10 years after the index was launched-occasioned no hoopla or analytical scrutiny.

The Wall Street Journal of the time quietly noted the closing level of the Dow Industrials-100.25-in a table. The day's lead article was about currency reform. The stock-market report talked about a "continuing bullish move" but made no mention of the industrial average.

Why the silence? Well, stocks were still considered speculative investments, industrial stocks particularly so. The blue chips of the day were railroads, and the industrial average, which began life in 1896 at the level of 40.94, hadn't yet caught on as the public's favorite stock-market barometer.

The stock market was extremely strong in late 1905, with the industrial average rising 17% in the fourth quarter as it approached the 100 mark. According to historian Robert Sobel, "the economy was going great guns," President Teddy Roosevelt was avidly pro-business, and the U.S. had won a ringing victory in the Spanish-American War. The economic boom was spurred partly by strong expansion in railroads, autos and steel, and partly by lingering stimulative effect from big gold discoveries in the Yukon and elsewhere.

Despite all of that, the Dow Jones industrials declined 2% for all of 1906, partly as a result of the San Francisco earthquake, a major investigation of the life-insurance industry by New York State, and anticipation of a 1907 recession.

Incidentally, While Dow industrials didn't make page one of the Journal on Jan. 13, 1906, a situation-wanted ad placed by a stenographer did. She was seeking a position with an established business, at a salary of $12 to $15 a week.

FIGURE 28—THE YANKEE-PENNAMITE WARS RESULTING IN THE CONNECTICUT CLAIM FROM SEA TO SEA

The geographic dispute started with a charter drawn for Conncticut by Charles II in 1662. The strip of land given to the state was supposed to extend "from sea to sea."

But later, the same king gave Pennsylvania founder William Penn land that overlapped with the Connecticut charter.

Three separate wares would follow.

In 1769, the Connecticut, Susquenhanna Co. sent its settler to the Wyoming Valley. They would eventually erect Fort Durkee on the river bank, near present-day Ross Street in Wilkes-Barre.

The company also established five townships-Wilkes-Barre, Nanticoke (now Hanover), Plymouth, Forty Fort (now Kingston) and Pittston.

For a time, the Connecticut settler dominated the local scene. They surveyed Wilkes-Barre and named the entire region Westmoreland. (The named lives on in Wilkes-Barre's Westmoreland Club). Officially the region was part of Litchfield County, Conn. Though it sat more than 200 miles away from the Constitution state.

Maj. John Durkee
TOWN PLANNER

Major John Durkee's 228-year-old plan to set aside a plot of land for public use still brings enjoyment to folks when they visit Downtown Wilkes-Barre.

Durkee, who named Wilkes-Barre after John Wilkes and Col. Isaac Barre, passionate supporters of the rights of American colonists, planned the map of Wilkes-Barre.

Durkee, president of the Susquehanna Company, a group of Connecticut settlers who migrated westward, began to plan the layout for Wilkes-Barre in 1770.

The design included a diamond-shaped center for town, now known as Public Square, where many still gather for festivities, such as the famous Farmers Market, which will begin its 25th season this June. A reserved site along the Susquehanna River, the River Common, is now commonly used to jog, bike, play games, and sunbathe when the weather is warm.

Durkee's original design of Wilkes-Barre was composed of 50 small family farms, and he set aside four acres as public space and more than 30 acres near the Susquehanna River.

In 1769, Durkee, who served as a colonel in one of Connecticut's regiments during the American Revolution, led 40 Connecticut Yankees into Wilkes-Barre and built a stockade, not far from what is now Ross Street, to the dislike of Pennsylvania authorities.

Battles erupted, and now a monument commemorates Fort Durkee, the first fort built by Connecticut settlers that was used during the first Yankee-Pennamite War in 1769. The plaque can be seen as one strolls down the path along the River Common.

Timothy Pickering
MEDIATOR

Born in 1745 to a well-to-do family in Salem, Mass., Timothy Pickering graduated from Harvard University and later pursued a career in law.

An advocate of American independence, Pickering served as quartermaster for Gen. George Washington's army.

He also made an impact in Northeastern Pennsylvania.

Pickering helped in the creation of Luzerne County, which was named for Chevalier La Luzerne, a one-time French minister to the United States.

He also was involved in the Yankee-Pennamite wars.

In 1662, England granted Connecticut colonists land in the northern half of Pennsylvania. Yet in 1681, William Penn was given a charter which included more than two-fifths of the land sold to the Connecticut settlers.

After much bloodshed and attempted compromise, Pickering had an idea. He proposed the New Englanders be allowed to retain their land, while Pennsylvanians be compensated with public lands elsewhere. Both sides eventually accepted his suggestion.

Pickering returned to Massachusetts, where he served as secretary of state and secretary of war, serving under President Washington. Later, he was elected as U.S. senator.

Pickering died in 1829.

Ellen Webster Palmer
SOCIAL REFORMER

The inscription on a statue of Ellen Webster Palmer describes her as "The Friend of the Working Boy."

And rightly so.

Palmer, mother of eight, was a breaker boy advocate.

Born in Plattsburg, N.Y., on Oct. 20, 1839, Palmer was the wife of Henry W. Palmer, a lawyer and Pennsylvania attorney general.

She made a difference in the lives of hundreds of youths by forming the Boys' Industrial Association in 1892.

Even though it was illegal, children as young as 8 were working in the coal mines as "breaker boys," sorting nonflammable slate from coal. Mine owners wanted cheap labor and the boys' families needed food and supplies to survive. Children worked a 10-hour day, six days a week.

With no time for education, the boys' futures didn't look promising. Palmer wanted to change that.

With community support, she started the BIA. The organization was designed to educate as well as entertain the breaker boys. Children learned reading, writing and arithmetic. Singing, debating and literacy clubs later formed.

The organization's first meetings were held in vacant stores. As the group's popularity spread, Wilkes-Barre City Council allowed it to use the fourth floor of City Hall. In 1899, the BIA constructed its own building behind City Hall, where the police station stands today.

Palmer died in 1918 at 78. The statue of her stands near the Luzerne County Courthouse.

Fell Tavern was razed in 1986

Historical marker to pay
tribute to Judge Jesse Fell

Consumer Price Index (CPI), All Items for All Urban Consumers, 1800-1998
and Producer Price Index (PPI), All Commodities, 1792-1998
(1967 = 100)

Source: Bureau of Labor Statistics, U.S. Department of Labor. Note: Prior to 1913, the CPI largely is based on prices for goods rather than goods and services, and on wholesale rather than retail prices. Annual data.

Courtesy of the Wyoming Historical and Geological Society

Spectators gather along the bank of the Susquehanna River as coal is loaded from Susquehanna Coal Co. breaker No. 13 to a canal boat in Plymouth Township. West Nanticoke was the end the North Branch Canal, which ran from the Wyoming Valley to Northumberland and ultimately Philadelphia. Extensions were added up river to Pittston. *Fig. 6*

Purchasing Power of Gold and of the Dollar
(1792 = 1.00)

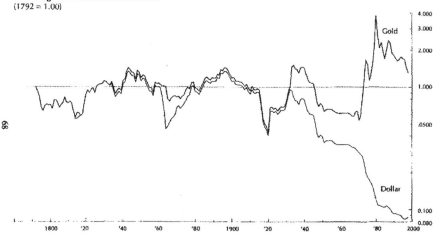

Note: On April 2, 1792, Congress established the dollar (then legally equivalent to 24.75 grains of pure gold) as the Nation's monetary unit. The changes in purchasing power shown in the chart were calculated from annual averages of the wholesale price index (source: U.S. Department of Labor) and the annual averages of the exchange ratio of dollars for gold.

219

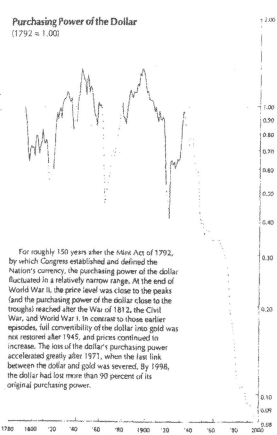

Purchasing Power of the Dollar
(1792 = 1.00)

For roughly 150 years after the Mint Act of 1792, by which Congress established and defined the Nation's currency, the purchasing power of the dollar fluctuated in a relatively narrow range. At the end of World War II, the price level was close to the peaks (and the purchasing power of the dollar close to the troughs) reached after the War of 1812, the Civil War, and World War I. In contrast to those earlier episodes, full convertibility of the dollar into gold was not restored after 1945, and prices continued to increase. The loss of the dollar's purchasing power accelerated greatly after 1971, when the last link between the dollar and gold was severed. By 1998, the dollar had lost more than 90 percent of its original purchasing power.

Note: Purchasing power was calculated from the Wholesale Price Index (source: Bureau of Labor Statistics, U.S. Department of Labor). The broken portions of the curve are periods when redeemability of the dollar into the monetary commodities at fixed rates was suspended.

1

The ole' breaker boys

Before labor laws were enacted, it was not unusual to see young boys journeying down into the mines, side-by-side with their fathers.

The youngest of these "breaker boys" toiled in the breakers. They sat on boards over sloping coal chutes and picked rock, slate and wood out of the chutes, all the while breathing the clouds of coal dust.

At 11, the boys tended to mules that hauled cars through the mine shafts. The older boys, 12 and older, went down in the cage to the deep mine shafts, started as door tenders, mule drivers, laborers and finally, miners.

This particular photo was taken some time during the 1890s.

As one could guess, the hazards associated with mine work were always prevalent. If you weren't caught in cave-ins or flash floods, you contracted mine asthma or black lung.

By 1960, the decline of coal as king had truly begun.

United Mine Workers President John Mitchell called on area miners to take on industrial giants

Before the strike of 1900, miners in Northeastern Pennsylvania were paid about $6.30 per day and were responsible for purchasing powder and paying their laborers. The strike won them a 63-cent-per-day raise.

Breaker boys: All work, no play and low pay

During the 1800s and early 1900s, life for many little boys in the Wyoming Valley was filled with a lot of hard work.

As young as seven and eight years old, the boys would work all day long at the coal breaker. By the time they got home late at night, there was little time left for play. They would eat, sleep and get ready for the next day's work.

As they got older, most breaker boys would follow in their father's and grandfather's footsteps by becoming miners.

According to the Lackawanna County Coal Mine, in 1902, breaker boys made 13 cents per hour. Also at that time, miners made approximately $2.75 per day, laborers, 18 cents per hour, and track layers, 24 cents per hour. Children also worked in the mining industry as slate pickers, making 6 cents per hour, and when they were a little older they made 13 cents per hour as mule drivers.

Photo, circa 1905, courtesy of Wyoming Historical and Geological Society.

President Teddy Roosevelt's pro-business stance and role in the U.S. victory in the Spanish-American War helped push the Dow over 100.

Bertha Robinson Conyngham
the wife of John N. Conyngham II

A polar bear mural hangs above Mr. Conyngham's former bathtub, now in the office of Ina K. Lubin, Penn State Wilkes-Barre's director of continuing education

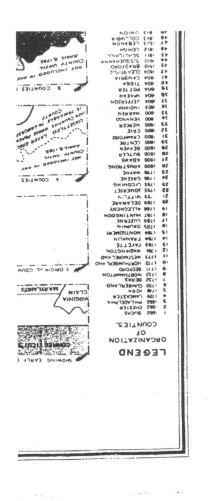

Hayfield House
the mansion of John N. Conyngham II

J. Pierpont MORGAN

J. Pierpont Morgan and his second wife, Fanny, in middle age.

MR Wright the Stepfather
Bertha Robinson Longyhore II

Mrs Wright the mother of
Bertha Robinson Conyngham
the Wife of John N. Conyngham II

Epilogue

WHAT DOES THE FUTURE HOLD FOR THE"
GREAT VALLEY" IN THE 21ST CENTURY?

Afterword

NO ONE EVEN TO THE PRESENT DAY ,BOTH IN NORTHEAST-
ERN PENNSYLVANIA OR THE UNITED STATES WAS AWARE OF
ALL THE THINGS DONE BOTH DELIBERATELY AND ACCIDEN-
TALLY TO BRING ABOUT THE INDUSTRIAL REVOLUTION. ONE
MAN "KING MORGAN" CONTROLLED THE ACTIONS OF ALL
THE MONEY MEN AND INDUSTRIAL POWERS TO BRING
ABOUT THE TREMENDOUS GROWTH DURING THE ANTHRACITE
COAL PERIOD OF 130 YEARS. WERE IT NOT FOR THE EQUITY
CONTRIBUTION (FROM COAL TRUSTS) IN NORTHEASTERN
PENNSYLVANIA NONE OF THIS GROWTH COULD HAVE TAKEN
PLACE.

About the Author

Thomas W. Dombroski the president of D & L Consultants (a management consulting firm) was graduated from King's College in Wilkes-Barre, Pa. And did graduate work at Wilkes University also in Wilkes-Barre. For ten years he was a senior process engineer with General telephone and Electronics Sylvania Electric Division in Towanda Pa. In 1965 he formed the management consulting firm. Mr. Dombroski has published Creative Problem Solving and taught the course at various public agencies to business men, social workers and community development personnel. He also taught his course over the radio station WRKC-FM. In addition he has a wide background in consulting services for small business in the commercial and industrial fields. During his career he participated in and helped complete various major industrial development projects in northeastern Pa that resulted in the completion of many infra structure improvements needed to bring about future industrial development in Northeastern Pa.

Thomas W. Dombroski is the president of D and L consultants enterprises incorporated (a management consulting firm) organized in Wilkes-Barre, PA. He graduated from King's College. He also completed graduate work at Wilkes University. For ten years he was a senior process engineer with General Telephone and Electronics in the Sylvania Electric Division located in Towanda, PA. In 1965, he formed his management consulting firm D&L Consultants. The author has taught a course in problem solving at various public agencies to businessmen, social workers, and community development personnel. He also taught his course over radio station WRKC in Wilkes -Barre, Pennsylvania. In addition, he has a wide background of experience in management consulting services especially for small businesses in the commercial and industrial fields. The author has previously published various papers during his engineering work and authored a book titled Creative Problem Solving. This new publishing venture covers the era from 1800 to 1999. It is a story about the financing of the United States of America. The story is titled, How America was financed. In this book the author explains how the discovery and presence of anthracite coal in Northeastern PA impacted on the people, the area, the environment, and the United States of America. In bringing this information together the author explains how anthracite coals financial proceeds and the shrewdness of the people who owned the coal lands combined to create great personal wealth, which was used to finance the United States of America, it's government and the industrial revolution through the financial and shrewd genius of one J.P. Morgan and his Northeast PA partners.

The author traces the discovery of anthracite coal on through the early 1800s through the Civil War, then through the industrial revolution and on through the First World War, through the second world war and on through the decline of anthracite coal, with the focus throughout being the analysis of the use of the tremendous wealth generated by the mining and sale of the anthracite coal.

This is a story of ambition, wealth, power, business acumen, and servitude. Thus leading to the establishment of the greatest financial power in the world both at the time of J. P. Morgan and the present time. The author blends fiction, fact, history, and speculation to bring out his story.

For Further Reading

1. HOVEY, CARL-THE LIFE STORY OF J. PIERPOINT MOR-GAN, NEW YORK; STURGIS AND WALTON CO., 1912

2. THE RICH AND THE SUPERRICH"A STUDY I THE POWER OF MONEY TODAY" COPYRIGHT 1968 BY FERDINAND LUNDBERG

3. PULITZER, A BIOGRAPHY, COPYRIGHT 1967 BY W. A. SWANBERG

4. FLAMES AND EMBERS OF COAL, COPYRIGHT 1990 BY ELLIS ROBERTS

5. THE FORDS, COPYRIGHT 1987 BY PETER COLLIER AND DAVID HOROWITZ

6. HISTORICAL ALBUM OF WILKES BARRE AND WYOMING VALLEY, COPYRIGHT 1976 BY WILBUR A. MYERS AND EDWARD HANLON PHD.

7. THOMAS, HUGH, 1931—THE SLAVE TRADE; THE STORY OF THE ATLANTIC SLAVE TRADE, 1440–1870/HUGH THOMAS, NEW YORK; SIMON AND SHUSTER, C. 1997

8. JOSEPHSON,. MATTHEW,1861-1901, HARCOURT AND BRACE, C1934, THE ROBBER BARONS—THE GREAT AMERICAN CAPITALISTS.

9. THE SUSQUEHANNA COMPANY PAPERS-PUBLISHED FOR THE WYOMING HISTORICAL AND GEOLOGICAL

SOCIETY-WILKES BARRE, PA.—PUBLISHED BY THE CORNELL UNIVERSITY PRESS, C1930.

10. CARSON, ANTHONY, PSEUD (i.e. PETER BROOKS), ON TO TIMBUCTOO, PUBLISHER, METHUEN AND CO.; LONDON, 1958

11. GLICKMAN, JAY L.—PAINTED IN BLOOD; REMEMBER WYOMING!, AMERICA'S FIRST CIVIL WAR, AFFILIATED WRITERS OF AMERICA, INC, C1997 (WYOMING VALLEY, PA. -HISTORY CODY WYOMING.

12. STROUSE, JEAN-MORGAN-AMERICAN FINANCER-RANDOM HOUSE, C1999

13. CARNEGIE, ANDREW—THE AUTOBIOGRAPHY OF ANDREW CARNEGIE, HOUGHTON MIFFLIN CO, C 1920

14. CONOT, ROBERT—A STREAK OF LUCK,THE LIFE AND LEGEND OF THOMAS ALVA EDISON,NEW YORK; SEAVIEW BOOKS, C1979

15. MEYER,BALTHASAR H.—A HISTORY OF THE NORTHERN SECURITIES CASE-BULLETIN OF THE UNIVERSITY OF WISCONSIN, NO. 142, MADISON, 1906

16. COTTER, ARUNDEL—THE AUTHJENTIC HISTORY OF THE UNITED STATES STEEL CORPORATION,NEW YORK; THE MOODY MAGAZINE AND BOOK CO, C1916

17. HARBAUGH,WILLIAM HENRY—THE LIFE AND TIMES OF THEODORE ROOSEVELT, NEW YORK; COLLIER BOOKS, 1963

18. KENNY, KEVIN-MAKING SENSE OF THE MOLLY MAGUIRES, NEW YORK, OXFORD UNIVERSITY PRESS, 1998

19. LETWIN, WILLIAM-LAW AND ECONOMOIC POLICY IN AMERICA, THE EVOLUTION OF THE SHERMAN ANTITRUST ACT, NEW YORK, RANDOM HOUSE, 1965

20. KLEIN, MAURY-JAY GOULD, BALTIMORE; JOHNS HOP-KINS UNIVERSITY PRESS, 1986
21. LIVINGSTON, JAMES-ORIGINS OF THE FEDERAL RESERVE SYSTEM; MONEY, CLASS, AND CORPORATE CAPITALISM 1890 T0 1913, ITHACA; CORNELL UNIVER-SITY PRESS, 1986
22. HOYT, EDWIN P. JR.—THE HOUSE OF MORGAN, NEW YORK; DODD, MEAD AND CO., 1966
23. THE JEWS OF WILKES BARRE IN WYOMING VALLEY (1845 TO 1995) MARJORIE LEVIN, JEWISH COMMUNITY CEN-TER OF WYOMING VALLEY, 1999